Scrumpy Dad

A Scrum Master's Guide to Happiness

Find your purpose to navigate the complexities of life

First published in 2023

ISBN 9789083383101

Edited by: Ameesha Green (The Book Shelf Ltd)

Cover design by: Peter Kuyt (Visual Friday)

Typeset by: Peter Kuyt (Visual Friday)

Illustrations by: Peter Kuyt (Visual Friday) and Herman Meeuwsen (Scrumpy Dad)

Proofread by: Gemma Rowlands (The Book Shelf Ltd)

www.scrumpydad.com

To my parents,
for their love, care and inspiration.

Contents

Introduction

No matter how unique we are as individual human beings regarding culture, beliefs, values, appearance, health, personality, age, and lifestyle, we share a common goal: the pursuit of happiness. However, happiness is a very subjective and personal concept, which means that each of us has to figure out what it means to us before we can pursue it.

Do you know what happiness looks like for you? Do you think you could be happier in certain areas of your life? Do you feel that life's challenges are blocking your path?

I can empathize, because I know this feeling very well. I struggled at home as a parent and husband a few years back. After a divorce, I remarried, and my two teenage kids from my former marriage stayed with us every weekend. They had to cope with different rules in each household because my ex-wife and I had different views on parenting. Since my kids were obviously loyal to their mother, they struggled to accept my new partner, whereas she was seriously trying to befriend them. This caused tangible friction when we were all together. I often felt and acted like the liaison officer in the middle of every argument about household chores or which television program to watch.

I felt responsible because I was the linking pin connecting their lives. I wanted to make it work for everybody but couldn't resolve this turbulent relationship between the three people I loved the most. They all seemed to accept this situation, but I was frustrated. I didn't want to continuously operate like a United Nations Blue Helmet, busy mediating, clarifying intentions, and ironing out misunderstandings. I knew there had to be a way to live together as a happy family. I wanted to nurture an environment with space for each of us as individuals, while also appreciating each other's company and having fun together. I didn't want to settle for anything less.

All of us face such challenges in our lives. Some challenges are big, and some are small. As children, we ideally receive love and support from our parents to get through the tough times. As we become teenagers, it gets tougher to navigate, and our parents try their best with all good intentions. They often have hardly any training or preparation, quickly leading to mistakes, tension, and conflict. Our challenges grow with us as we age, and work challenges are added to the equation. Challenges are considered part of the job when it comes to work, and we often get professional help from trainers, mentors, and coaches to cope with them. This helps us to become successful at work. By contrast, we lack such support in facing the challenges in our personal lives. Ironically, some of the biggest challenges in life can come from our personal issues, be it divorce, family problems, or losing loved ones.

These challenges ultimately come down to the pursuit of happiness – or, more specifically, how we can be happy or happier given our situation, job, relationships, or life in general. But what does happiness look like, and how do we grasp it? Surprisingly enough, the answer to this is pretty straightforward: happiness is what each of us determines it to be, and the way we achieve it is to choose more of what makes us happy. Because external and internal factors so easily influence happiness, it is often a temporary experience, so how can we maintain a more steady and enduring state of happiness?

I define happiness as a state of joyful wellbeing where you realize you are content with what you experience. It can be invoked by what you do or think. Happiness is closely related to our needs, values, and purpose, because when our needs are fulfilled, we feel happy since we have what we longed for. It feels great when we can express our values through our actions and realizing that our life aligns with our purpose is an incredible experience.

Of course, throughout life, we are faced with questions that influence our happiness. Which type of education should I choose? Which job fits my talents and ambitions? How do I balance my work life and private life? How do I stay healthy? How do I find a partner? How do I keep my relationships interesting? How do I stay loyal to my own ambitions? How do I stay focused and committed in the face of setbacks? How do I deal with significant life events such as illness, conflict, crime, or the death of a loved one? We are all looking for answers to such questions, and we all have to make our own decisions to lead us towards happiness.

The significant constraint is that we only have one life, and our time is limited. Because there is so much to do, so much we want, and so much that is expected of us, it's impossible to have it all. Life is a constant balancing act of time and energy. We can maximize that time and leverage our energy to make us and those around us as happy as possible. I realized it while working as a Scrum Master, as odd as that might sound.

Scrum Master is an accountability defined in Scrum[1]. Scrum is a framework providing guidelines for teams to work successfully together when operating in complex environments, i.e., where most information is unknown, and many uncertainties exist. By experimenting and organizing work in short cycles, teams learn by doing, while maintaining the ability to adapt quickly to new insights, experiences or unforeseen events.

Agile is the mindset reflected in the values and principles as captured in the Agile Manifesto[2]. It thrives on a culture of close collaboration, empowerment and autonomy, technical excellence and value for customers, among other aspects.

Over the past 15-20 years, many organizations worldwide adopted Scrum to foster such an Agile culture. It helped them move away from the unfit industrial way of working. It supported them to deal timely and effectively with inevitable changes, focus on customer value, minimize waste, and to continuously improve. Many practices and tools have been developed over time to support this way of working. Although both Scrum and Agile have their roots in software product development, their adoption has spread to many other domains beyond IT, demonstrating the need for such a more suitable way of working.

A Scrum Master supports individuals, teams and organizations working with the Scrum framework to enable them to be most effective in delivering valuable products and services to users, resulting in benefits to the organization represented by its stakeholders. Being a Scrum Master isn't easy. As the Scrum Guide used to state, Scrum is lightweight, simple to understand, and difficult to master. Reading and understanding the Scrum Guide[1] is the first step, but genuinely upholding the Scrum Master accountabilities while serving everybody involved is no mean feat. It took me years to fully understand the ins & outs of the Scrum Master role. The more experienced I became, the more I realized how much I still had to learn.

In this book you will learn to build a happier life for you and your loved ones based on proven Scrum Master practices. First, you'll learn to clarify your personal goals, values, and purpose; then, you'll learn how to take advantage of your strengths and be aware of your weaknesses. Next, you'll discover an effective method to consciously choose, plan, and execute your actions, and finally apply powerful evaluation techniques to check your progress and adjust your plan when needed. Along the way, you'll develop the flexibility to deal with change, setbacks, and unknowns and improve yourself continuously. Plus, you'll get plenty of practices, tools, and easy-to-use templates to support you.

I saw first-hand the value of these methods when I organized a constructive meeting with my kids and my partner, inspired by the power of Scrum's retrospective event. The meeting format allowed us to talk openly and honestly about our personal values, needs, and struggles. As a result, our mutual understanding deepened. We all loved the experience, and our communication started to improve. We grew closer as a family, which made us all happier. I cover this family retrospective in more detail in the chapter 'Checking your course'.

And so, I learned that Agile and Scrum practices can be a great inspiration to use at home. I started writing on Medium under the nickname Scrumpy Dad to share these valuable experiences with others. Encouraged by the positive responses, I crafted the essential stories into a book. Consider this book your personal guide and Do-It-Yourself (DIY) manual to get a grip of your life and become happier through proven Scrum Master practices.

However, like any book and like Scrum itself, this is not the silver bullet to personal success. This book will help you on your journey of making life easier and increasing your chances of success and happiness. Be aware that this book is not an instruction manual on fully implementing Scrum at home, according to the Scrum Guide. Ultimately, it's up to you to take action, experiment, recover from setbacks, learn from mistakes, and adapt your plans to reach your personal goals. My ambition is to share helpful insights, practices and tools that offer value.

The real trick here is to find what works for you and implement it to make your life happier. These hands-on practices are easy to apply, so you will quickly learn how to use them and reap the benefits. Oh, and it really helps if you've got some A3 and A4 paper and different color sticky notes. Are you ready to become the Scrum Master of your life and pursue happiness?

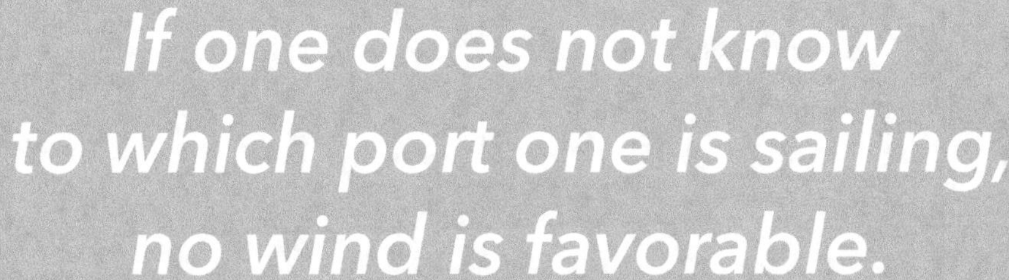

*If one does not know
to which port one is sailing,
no wind is favorable.*

\- Seneca

Steering towards happiness

Since the start of my career, I have been intrigued by productivity tools to help me organize my work. I have used to-do lists, spreadsheets, paper calendars, gadgets, apps, and anything that gave me control over my long, diverse list of tasks. I liked it so much that I started using these tools for personal tasks like home chores, holiday preparation, DIY projects, etc. These tools helped me manage all the work to be done at home and plan which task to execute when.

Sometimes, it got out of hand: the time spent planning and organizing got in the way of actually doing the work. Next to the waste of time, I got frustrated about the rut of planning tasks, rescheduling delayed tasks, and ticking off tasks that were done. This tedious administration was taking its toll. I completed tasks but needed more motivation to keep going. After some self-reflection, I realized I was so focused on managing my tasks that I had forgotten why these tasks mattered to me in the first place. I needed to find my purpose to keep me motivated and feel happy about the progress I was making!

While pondering my purpose, I realized that this is precisely what we do in teambuilding workshops when creating new teams. As a Scrum Master, I regularly facilitate workshops based on the so-called Team Canvas[3]. It is a canvas to help teams align on their way of working in order to achieve their team goals. At the heart of the canvas is the team's purpose. I imagined this approach could work out equally well for individuals like you and me at home. So, I adapted the Team Canvas to make it fit for personal use and called it the Steering Wheel because I realized it was like the steering wheel of a sailing boat. During personal development training a long time ago, I experienced guided meditation about taking control of your own life. This was symbolized by taking the steering wheel of a sailing boat in your hands and navigating that boat through a heavy storm. The sailing boat symbolizes your life, and the steering wheel is the tool to help you steer towards happiness. During your journey, you will encounter setbacks, surprises and everything else that life throws at you. When you keep your hands firmly on the steering wheel, you can make it through.

If you want to find happiness in your life, it's good to know what happiness looks like for you personally. Your definition of happiness is influenced by your upbringing, experiences, and cultural norms of the various groups you identify with. Nowadays, social media plays an important role, too. Every minute of the day, you can see on your phone a rose-tinted version of what your life could look like. Or at least that's how others share their definition of happiness.

However, to find happiness, you need to look inside yourself because you are the starting point for your journey:

- What is it that you want to achieve?
- Which values matter to you?
- What is your purpose in life?
- Which strengths can you put into practice?
- What are your weaknesses to be aware of?

In this chapter, you learn how to use the Steering Wheel tool to answer these questions. It will help you understand yourself better to increase your chances of succeeding on your terms. Let's have a closer look at the Steering Wheel and how this can work for you.

Navigating your life towards happiness.

Preparation

First, get yourself a large sheet of paper, at least A3, or 2 sheets of A4 stuck together with some tape. You can also put 4 A4 sheets together for an even larger working space if you want. Draw your Steering Wheel as large as possible on the sheet.

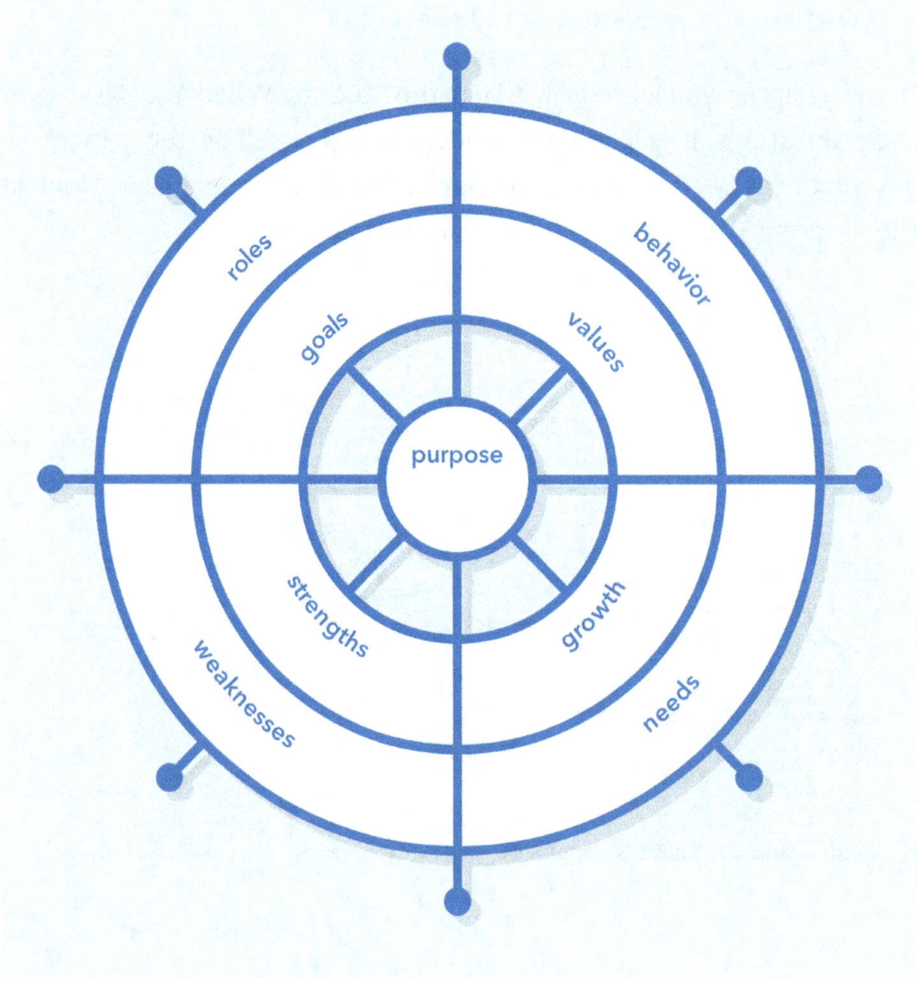

Steering Wheel template.

Now it's time to fill out your Steering Wheel. For each section, I will provide an explanation and instructions to complete this process.

Roles

In this section, list the various roles you play in life and write them on sticky notes. Are you a parent? That's one role. In a relationship? Then you are a partner, lover, or whatever applies to you. You likely play the role of a family member and friend too. And what about your hobbies? Maybe you play a role as a trainer or coach for the local sports club. Or are you a volunteer for a charity organization on the weekend?

Think of the various environments where you show up. You'll discover that you play plenty of roles in your life, some more demanding or time-consuming than others. As a result, you will need to divide your time and energy between your roles. Some roles will be more important to you than others. Therefore, you may want to focus on those roles first to increase your happiness. Identifying all your roles in life helps you to choose where to pursue happiness first.

Because work-life quickly overloads private life, I solely focus on personal roles in this exercise. Of course, it is perfectly fine to include your professional roles as well in your Steering Wheel; that is up to you.

Goals

Setting goals adds meaning to your life. Goals also provide hope and motivation. And it feels good when you make progress on your goals, let alone achieve your goals. All these factors contribute to your happiness. Which goals do you want to achieve in the upcoming timeframe, say one year from now? Those goals are typically related to one of your roles. Make it personal and list them here.

Support yourself by formulating your goals in a **SMART** way:

- **Specific**: enough detail so it is clear what you mean.
- **Measurable**: to make sure you can determine your progress and final state.
- **Ambitious**: maybe a bit uncomfortable, but definitely inspiring to work on.
- **Realistic**: it can be done (even if you don't know how yet).
- **Timely**: to have a point in time to focus your efforts.

Keep in mind that formulating these goals will help you find direction. As I can personally testify, some goals will ultimately prove to be more successful than others. That doesn't make it less valuable to strive for them all equally.

Some examples of my personal goals over the past years:

- As a homeowner, I want to renovate the ground floor of our house so that we can enjoy our new kitchen with easy access to the garden this summer.
- As a writer, I want to find a publisher for my book on my divorce by the end of this calendar year so that others can benefit from my lessons learned.
- As a dad, I want to organize a fun event with my partner this spring to spend quality time with our kids.

You may have noticed that I use a particular format to describe my goals. It is inspired by the User Story format that Scrum teams often apply as a good practice:

As a <role>, I want <personal goal to be achieved> so that
<valuable outcome>.

By specifying the <role>, the relevant context of the goal is immediately apparent. What I like even better is the <valuable outcome> part. This part emphasizes the underlying motivation to reach the goal, the outcome you want to achieve, and why it matters to you. Working with SMART goals may become dull over time. The <valuable outcome> part constantly reminds you why this goal matters to you. It helped me stay inspired and find new energy when encountering setbacks.

How many goals you want to set for yourself is up to you. Some goals will be small and take only a few weeks, whereas other goals may take a full year or more to complete. When you look at your list of goals, you should have the feeling that it can be done in the given timeframe, if all works out well. Your goals might feel challenging and should still motivate you to go for it. If you feel overwhelmed by your goals, it's better to adjust your ambition and choose fewer or smaller goals.

Values

Values are the beliefs or principles that define what you find important in your life. Values are at the core of your personality. Values drive your behavior. They act as a moral compass, often unknowingly, when you make important decisions in life. When you live in line with your values, you will feel content and happy. When your life is not aligned with your values, it will feel wrong, even to the point that you feel miserable. So, which values define you at the core? Which values are so fundamental to you that they are non-negotiable?

Here are a few ways to go about this exercise.

Picklist

Look at the list of values provided in this chapter. Browse the list and write down those values that resonate with you. Trust your gut feeling here. You'll likely end up with a long list. Now, cluster these values together in groups of related values. For each group, choose one value that best describes the values in that group, and which appeals to you most. Now you have a shortlist. Pick the top 3 values that you care about most.

TIP

Please note that this list is a selection of most common personal values provided for your inspiration. When you find a different value that is not on this list, that is perfectly fine. This exercise is about you discovering your values.

Accountability	Exploration	Mindfulness
Adventure	Fairness	Open-mindedness
Altruism	Faith	Optimism
Ambition	Family	Patience
Authenticity	Flexibility	Peace
Balance	Forgiveness	Perseverance
Belonging	Freedom	Playfulness
Bliss	Friendship	Positivity
Boldness	Fun	Purpose
Calmness	Generosity	Quality
Challenge	Gratitude	Resilience
Change	Growth	Respect
Charity	Happiness	Responsibility
Collaboration	Harmony	Security
Commitment	Health	Self-discipline
Compassion	Honesty	Service
Confidence	Hope	Simplicity
Connection	Humility	Spirituality
Courage	Independence	Stability
Creativity	Inner peace	Strength
Curiosity	Integrity	Teamwork
Determination	Intuition	Thoughtfulness
Diversity	Kindness	Tolerance
Empathy	Leadership	Trust
Empowerment	Learning	Understanding
Equality	Love	Unity
Excellence	Loyalty	Wisdom

Past experiences

Another approach is to think back to your best moments in life, when you felt most happy, proud or satisfied. Relive that experience and ask yourself: what made me feel that way back then? Which values were fulfilled? Use the provided list of values to pick those values that resonate the most with your experience. This approach works the same with bad moments and conflicts. In that case, which values were neglected or at stake? Write down these values.

Inspirational people

Who are your heroes in life? Which people, dead or alive, inspire you? It does not have to be an international celebrity, it might just as well be somebody close to you, like a friend or family member. Which qualities do you admire in them? Could that be a value that is important to you? Write it down.

> **TIP**
>
> *Don't go overboard, listing all values that resonate with you. Limit yourself to 3–5 values that really drive you.*

Behavior

Having your values defined is a great start. These values constitute your moral compass and they provide guidance to live by. You feel great when your life is aligned with your values, but values are very much internal which means nobody can see them. Our values become visible in our behavior when others can hear what we say and see what we do.

To support yourself in living in line with your values, it is essential to have a concrete idea of how your values show up in your behavior.

For each of your values, ask yourself:

- How do I express myself when I am truly living this value?
- How do I behave?
- What do I do in particular situations?
- What can others see me doing when I express my values?

Write down your behavior in the format: If **<situation>**, then **<behavior>**.

This helps to remind yourself to practice this **<behavior>** when that **<situation>** occurs. It also provides some context for you to specify your intended behavior. I have provided some of my personal values and behavior as an example.

Value	Behavior
Inspiration	If I discover an interesting new topic, I bookmark it so I can look it up later.
	If a story touches me, I share it with others (writing or telling).
Openness	If I feel the need to share what I experience, then I will speak up even if it's uncomfortable.
	If I get into a debate with somebody, then I keep asking questions to understand their point of view.
Integrity	If I promise something, then I commit to do what I said.
Fun	Every day I make sure I take a moment to enjoy the present.
	I organize outings with my family to spend quality time together.

> **TIP**
>
> *Start with one of the roles you identified earlier. Imagine how you would behave in that role when fully expressing one of your values. This helps to come up with behavior that corresponds to that value.*

Purpose

This is your personal mission statement, your higher goal in life, the reason you want to get out of bed in the morning. Having a purpose provides you with focus and meaning for taking action. You feel that your contribution matters, not just to yourself but also to others. You feel connected to something bigger than yourself. As a result, when you can align your actions with your purpose, you will feel happier.

Now we get to the heart of the matter. Looking at your roles, goals, and values: which life-fulfilling ambition or dream comes to mind? That is an easy question to ask, but a tough one to answer, so here are a few practical exercises to choose from to help you define your purpose. Be aware that this section of the Steering Wheel is by far the toughest part, because it is so fundamental to your being. Take your time, as this is your purpose and offers valuable guidance on your life journey.

Choose the method that most appeals to you. Then, just invest the time you need to complete the exercise. Figuring out your purpose is something you will only do occasionally in your life, so it's important to do it right. Your future self will thank you.

Purpose diagram

The Purpose diagram describes three main areas that should be covered to find your purpose: what you love, what you are good at, and what the world needs. Your purpose combines all three areas into one. As such, it is a simplified version of the Ikigai-diagram[4].

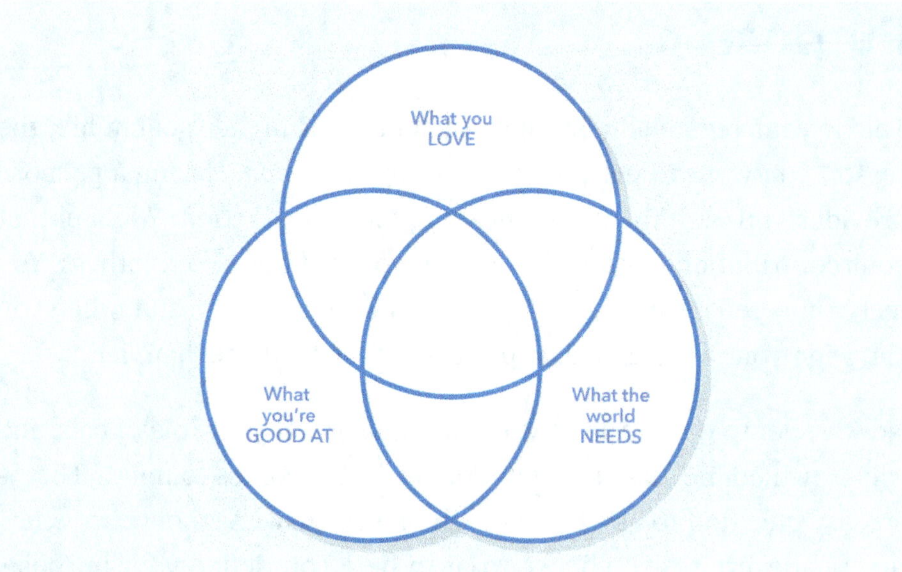

Purpose diagram template.

Step 1.

First, get yourself a large sheet of paper, at least A3 or 2 sheets of A4 stuck together. You can also put 4 A4 sheets together for an even larger working space if you want.

Step 2.

Draw the Purpose diagram.

Step 3.

Take the following questions one by one and write the answers on sticky notes and put these in the related circle:

- What are you **GOOD AT**?
- What do you **LOVE**?
- What does the world **NEED**?

Step 4.

Look where two circles overlap and figure out what the related sticky notes have in common. Write all of this down on new sticky notes and put them in the appropriate overlapping areas:

- Your **PASSION** = what you love and what you are good at.
- Your **MISSION** = what the world needs that you love.
- Your **VOCATION** = what you are good at that the world needs.

You can also get creative by joining items from the individual circles into new combinations. From there, you can elaborate further to discover even more options.

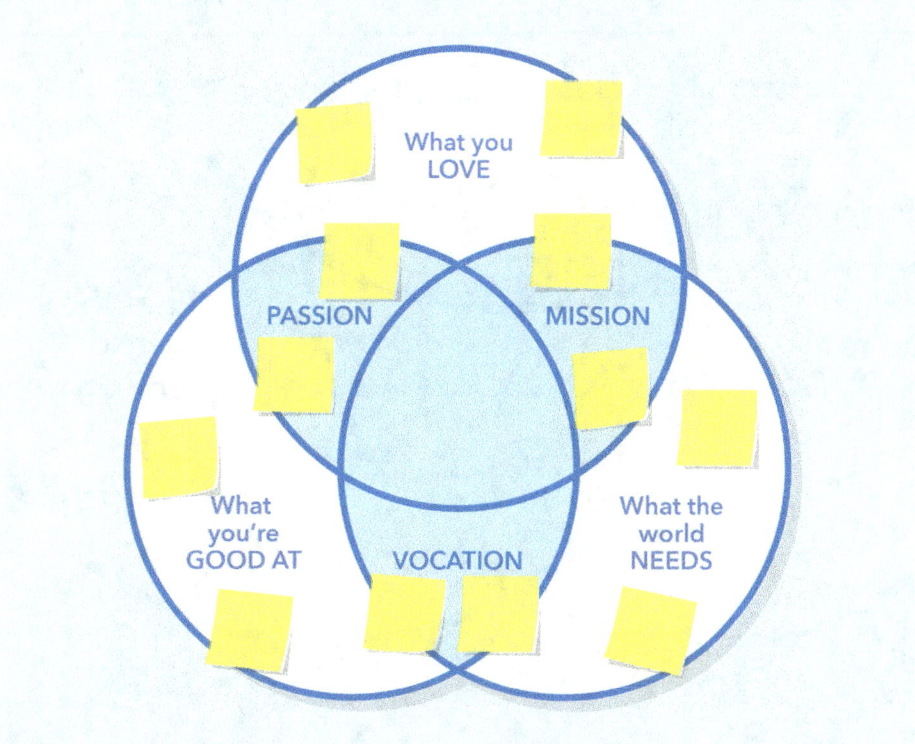

Passion, Mission, and Vocation in the Purpose diagram.

Example of a completed Purpose diagram.

Step 5.

In the center of the diagram, all 3 circles overlap, this is your sweet spot. Mix and match the results from the previous step into new combinations. Refine these results until you find an answer to all 3 questions. Formulate this as one sentence. This is your purpose.

You may not be too pleased with the first version of your purpose. That is okay. It is perfectly fine to start off with an initial version. Take a break or get a good night's sleep. Revisit your purpose and refine it further until you are happy about it. When you feel good about what you crafted, you found your purpose, it works for you. Excellent!

> **TIP**
>
> *In this exercise we focus on finding your purpose in your personal life by defining what you are good at, what you love to do, and what the world needs. If you want to extend your purpose to your professional life, you need to ask yourself one more question: what can I be paid for? This is called finding your Ikigai[4].*

Word association

Start writing down words and phrases that motivate you. You may have some favorite quotes or sayings that are meaningful to you. Then, start combining and rewriting these bits and pieces into new phrases. In the end, forge these phrases together into a sentence. Initially, this will be a long sentence that may feel a bit artificial. Rewrite and finetune it until you have composed your own purpose in one inspiring sentence.

End in mind

This exercise comes from Stephen Covey's great book *The 7 Habits of Highly Effective People*[5]. Habit #2 is called "Begin with the end in mind". Ask yourself this question: how would you like to be remembered? How would you like people to talk about you when you are no longer there? It is a bit confrontational to ponder about what you want to leave behind, but answering this question will help you find your purpose.

When I reflect on my own mortal existence, I hope that people remember me as somebody who inspired them to try out new ways to create happiness in their lives. That starts with being a loving partner for my spouse and a caring parent for my kids. Next, I share my stories with family, friends and colleagues. From there, I want to reach more people. So, you can see where this book is coming from.

> **TIP**
>
> *Write your purpose in the present tense. It's not just an intention for the future. Start living your purpose today!*

Strengths

Now it's time to be honest about your personal strengths. Which competencies, skills, and experience do you possess that will support you in achieving your goals and purpose? Again, there are a few ways to go about it.

Self-reflection

Your strengths will typically show up in various areas of your life. Your strengths define you. Think back on your achievements so far: at home, at work, at sports, at charity, in the various roles that you play in your life.

Questions to ask yourself:

- Which personal qualities am I proud of?
- What am I good at?
- What do other people like about me?
- What do other people compliment me for?
- How could I help others?

Don't be modest, and list everything that comes to mind.

Ask for feedback

If you find it difficult to identify your own strengths, ask somebody close to you to give you input, like a friend, your partner or a colleague. It should be somebody who knows what you are capable of and has seen you in action.

Questions you could ask:

- What do you see as my strong points or hidden talents?
- What am I good at?
- What do you like about me?
- What kind of help could I provide to you or others?
- What makes me standout from other people?

- How would you describe me to others?

Make sure to ask them for specific examples so it is clear to you what they mean.

Superhero

Get creative and imagine yourself in a cool outfit with unique superpowers. Get paper and pencils out and draw yourself as a new superhero. Finish it off with a cool name too! Now what are your superpowers, dear superhero? There you have your strengths.

I discovered I'm pretty creative in twisting my mind to incorporate new ideas into my routines, so I call myself Mind Bender.

Weaknesses

People often find it more natural to focus on their weaknesses rather than their strengths, so this section could be easier. Be honest but also kind to yourself. Just face the fact that we are all human and have some flaws we are not proud of.

Self-reflection

Think back of unpleasant activities or struggles from the past. Forget about the circumstances and focus on yourself. Which personal characteristics made it tough for you? What are you not good at? What don't you like? What do you feel uncomfortable about and what would you like to stay away from? These are your weaknesses.

Ask for feedback

If you have asked somebody for input on your strengths, go ahead and ask them about your weaknesses too. If they care and dare enough, they can help out here. You might have to encourage them to be really open and honest with you. It's generally easier to give a compliment than to share constructive criticism.

Superhero

If you drew yourself as a superhero: what would your Achilles heel be? All superheroes have a weak spot or a vulnerability. For Superman it's kryptonite. What are your weaknesses?

Opposite forces

Your biggest strengths can also be your weaknesses in certain situations. Take a look at your strengths and ask yourself: what happens when I overdo it? What are the unintended side-effects when I deploy my strengths to the max?

Growth

Take a look at your Steering Wheel so far. Do you need any new competencies or skills to meet your goals and live your purpose? Which strengths should you build out further? Are there any weaknesses you need to address to be successful? In the Growth section of the Steering

Wheel, you can list all your ideas for training, workshops, courses, coaching, and books on topics where you want to improve.

Needs

Take a look at the sections Goals, Purpose, and Growth on your Steering Wheel. Now ask yourself: which resources do I need to achieve all this? Think of materials, information, help, support, environment, budget, or anything else that you need to succeed. Write that down in the Needs section to take care of it later and set yourself up for success.

Final check

To complete the Steering Wheel, let's do a final check to see if it is complete and consistent. Browse through all the sections and check the following:

- Is what you wrote here clear to you? Will it still make sense when you reread this in a few weeks or months from now? Make sure you will still understand afterward.
- Is there something important missing? Only add stuff that adds value.
- Is there something that can be removed? Is there too much? Remove stuff that doesn't add up or seems less relevant now you look at the whole picture.

Example of a completed Steering Wheel.

Using the Steering Wheel

There is another very practical question to be answered: Where will you keep your personal Steering Wheel? Are you going to put it physically on a wall somewhere? Or keep it as a digital version on your laptop or mobile? Put your Steering Wheel in a place that can serve as a visual reminder. Especially in the beginning when your purpose, goals, values and other sections are still fresh and need to sink in.

You don't need to actively maintain the Steering Wheel. I recommend reviewing your Steering Wheel at least once a year, or when major changes occur in your life. Strengths and weaknesses may have changed as you have grown as a person and gained more experience. You might have accomplished some of your goals, or new ones have popped up. Maybe your roles changed. Update your Steering Wheel as needed. That also holds for your values and purpose, although these will be less subject to change as they are so fundamental to you as a person. We will cover this in the chapter 'Checking your course'.

When I completed this Steering Wheel exercise for myself, it gave me excellent insights into where I wanted to go. I used the Purpose Diagram and had a fun session producing plenty of sticky notes. I realized how much I love to write and share stories. I am also good at writing (at least I think so). Publishing blogs and books can make some money. Last but not least, the world can benefit from more love and happiness. My purpose is to inspire others to create happiness in their lives by sharing personal experiences. And that is why you are reading this book right now.

Share your Steering Wheel with somebody close to you, like your partner or a good friend. I'm confident they are keen to learn what you find important in your life, so be open about it. It is very likely that they want to support you, and by being open about your purpose, values, and goals, you invite them to share their plans and dreams too. That might just lead to a beautiful conversation.

Several months later I had the opportunity to apply the Steering Wheel again, this time for my partner. She was studying and looking for a new job. She knew that she needed to make a different choice than before. She wanted to break the pattern of previous administrative jobs in real estate that did not make her happy. I helped her fill out the Steering Wheel and we had some great conversations.

She discovered that one of her strengths (sorting out a complex administrative mess) was often not appreciated in the type of jobs she had worked before. With the various new insights, she was able to redirect her job-hunting quest. Eventually, she found a nice job in the workforce staffing industry where her strength was needed and appreciated. For the first time in many years, she didn't get frustrated after the first half year, but started to enjoy her job.

The Steering Wheel is a great tool, not only for yourself but also to help others gain more insight about themselves. As a parent, you can support your adolescents with this tool. They face serious challenges like choosing whether, how and where to continue their education. Or maybe they are considering a first job. You don't have to complete the whole exercise. Just starting the conversation about strengths and weaknesses, growth, and needs could already be good inspiration.

Summary

In this chapter, you have learned about the Steering Wheel and how it serves you to take your life in your hands on your journey towards happiness. It helps to focus on what matters most to you. The most important part is at its center: your purpose.

The Steering Wheel sections are:

- **Roles**: the various roles you play in your life.
- **Goals**: the personal objectives you want to achieve.
- **Values**: your moral compass.
- **Behavior**: how you express your values.
- **Purpose**: your north star, a stable beacon that guides you on your journey.
- **Strengths**: your best competencies, skills, and qualities that will help you succeed.
- **Weaknesses**: underdeveloped competencies or qualities that may hinder you.
- **Growth**: your personal development that will help you reach your goals.
- **Needs**: the resources you need to arrange to be successful.

The Steering Wheel provides a grip on your life. Take your time to fill it out and clarify all these aspects using the exercises provided because it's all about you and how you want to live your life and find happiness. The Steering Wheel is crucial to bootstrap your next steps in achieving your goals and living your purpose.

In the next chapters, we will be looking at planning and execution to reach your goals and explore helpful routines to check your course and adjust if needed because life is always full of surprises.

*If you are not working on
your own perfect day,
you are working on
somebody else's.*

- Stephen Covey

Planning your journey

As a Scrum Master I guide teams to work with the Scrum framework, where they plan actions in detail in the short term in order to reach longer term goals. New work and insights are discovered as they go. The framework supports them to quickly adapt their plan of action when circumstances change (and they always do).

Many Scrum teams use a physical or digital board to visualize their work. It creates transparency for everybody by showing the work in its current state. It is a great tool to keep an overview of all work to be done and is used by Scrum teams to review their progress on a daily basis. As a Scrum Master I facilitate this recurring inspection and adaptation process so the team can stay most effective.

Wouldn't it be great if we could benefit from such a helpful tool for our own goals at home, too? That's why I've created my own personal task board using a similar format. This board shows what I need to do today, this week, and this month. It also keeps me aware of how all of my actions push me toward my personal goals. I call it the Journey Planner.

Over time, I experienced several benefits of using this Journey Planner:

- I found it very helpful to have one clear overview of my most important goals and all related actions. Everything that is important to me is on there, which provides peace of mind. It also helps when prioritizing because it is all there and I can oversee the impact of reshuffling actions, resulting in fewer surprises.

- By choosing what is most important today, I am focused on what matters now.

- When actions are not moving, I know I need to do something different to tackle frustration.

- Full columns are a visual indicator that I am planning too many actions, so I can steer away from overloading myself.

- It feels great to put an action to done, getting yet another step closer to a goal.

In this chapter you'll learn how to use the Journey Planner to make the Steering Wheel actionable, because planning and actions are needed to make things happen in the real world. The Journey Planner supports you in your journey towards happiness because it helps you stay focused and loyal to the goals that matter so much to you despite the circumstances.

Here's how to make your own Journey Planner.

Preparation

First, get yourself a large sheet of paper, preferably A3, or 2 sheets of A4 stuck together. If you have a whiteboard, that is fine too. Next, draw your Journey Planner as large as possible on the sheet with six columns: **Goals**, **To do**, **This month**, **This week**, **Today** and **Done**.

Goals	To do	This month	This week	Today	Done

Journey Planner template.

Enter your goals

In the first column, you enter your goals. These are typically important personal projects that you want to start working on. Look at the Goals section on your Steering Wheel, and select those goals you want to plan actions for in the short term (coming weeks). If you have some goals that do not require immediate action yet, please leave them for later. Starting planning too early is wasting time.

Write your goals to be planned on colored sticky notes, choose a color per goal. Rank them from most to least important. This will help later on when you have to choose how to spend your time most effectively.

Plan your actions

Identify the actions needed to achieve each goal. Write each action on a separate sticky note in the color that's chosen for the specific goal. If you don't have colored sticky notes, you can also arrange your goals and related actions in horizontals lanes on your board.

One of the key ingredients of successful planning and execution is to make your actions as concrete as possible. Use the format "verb + noun" to make it actionable. For instance, "write newsletter draft", "send birthday gift" or "call building contractor".

Ideally, each action should be something you can complete in one day. If not, break it down into smaller actions. There is nothing more frustrating than looking at a task that is stuck in the **Today** column for days on end because it takes so long to complete.

Move your actions around. Decide whether your actions should be completed this month, this week, or today. If actions can wait, put them in the **To do** column. This is your backlog for the near future (next month or later).

Here are some basic guidelines on planning:

- **Choose the order**: Some actions need to happen in a particular sequence. Put them vertically on the board in that order and start working your way down when picking them up. For my renovation projects, there is typically some tearing down work to do first, then some new construction work, and finally decorating.

- **Plan backward**: Certain preliminary actions may take time, so take that into account and plan backward. In order to renovate the ceiling in our kitchen, I needed to take into account delivery times of all the materials. So, I knew by which date I had to place the orders to have all materials delivered in time to start the work.

- **Be aware of deadlines**: Some actions have strict due dates: there might be a deadline you need to be aware of or an event that you are preparing for. Tax papers need to be filed, you want to prepare for that party next weekend, and the dustbins must be on the street tomorrow morning. Hence, due dates are an important aspect to take into account when choosing which actions to pick up when. But remember, it is always your choice to comply with a deadline or not (and accept the consequences). Write the due date on the sticky note so you can take that into account when planning. Because we had ordered an entire new kitchen to be installed by the supplier, I had a very definite deadline to finish my work.

- **Plan dependencies**: For some actions you are dependent on somebody else to provide you with something you need. Split that up into separate actions for ease of planning. We needed an electrician to upgrade our fuse box to cater for the new induction cooker. I created actions for specifying our needs, making an appointment with the electrician, and preparing the wiring.

Be realistic about what you can achieve. You don't need one action for each goal in your **Today** column. Don't overload yourself. We often overestimate what we can achieve in the short term and underestimate what we can accomplish in the long term (Gates' Law).

> **TIP**
>
> *Put today's actions as reminders in your phone calendar to allocate time for them and have an alert go off.*

Using the Journey Planner

When you complete an action, move it to the **Done** column. Make sure to celebrate the achievement! It is too easy to take stuff for granted, so be proud of every action you complete.

Create daily, weekly and monthly habits to review your Journey Planner and adjust your planning where needed. Can one of your **This week** actions be moved to **Today**? Should an action from **This month** move to **This week** or even **Today**? Maybe an unfinished action from **Today** has become less urgent and should be moved to **This month**?

At any time, you might discover that new actions arise, or that a particular action is too big and can be split up into smaller actions that can be executed separately. Create sticky notes for these new actions and put them in the appropriate column with the relevant goal.

Regularly, take a step back and quickly check if your goals still have the same priority. If not, adjust the order of your goals accordingly on your Journey Planner. You should also check your remaining goals on your Steering Wheel. It might be time to act on them and start including new goals into your planning. If you include these checks in your monthly habit, you should be fine.

Whatever the situation, update your Journey Planner to reflect the latest status in order to feel confident about your planning.

<table>
<tr><th>Goals</th><th>To do</th><th>This month</th></tr>
<tr>
<td>

Aging healthy

Best husband for my wife

Best dad for my kids

Publish Scrumpy Dad book

Enjoy golf & improve my game

Do charity work

</td>
<td>

Plan spa resort trip

Plan family event in December

Organize launch party

Plan training sessions

Meet in person

</td>
<td>

Monthly retro together

Fix lighting for Valerie

Submit final version

</td>
</tr>
</table>

This week | Today | Done

This week

- Early morning yoga on weekdays
- Dinner with Maaike
- Order DIY materials
- Review Acknowledgements
- Complete Print On Demand intake
- Practice putting

Today

- Reduce coffee intake
- Drink 2,5L water
- Call Bart

Done

- Buy flowers
- Launch website
- Review Dutch text

My first personal Journey Planner started as a physical board on the wall in the hallway next to our bedroom. I walked past it every morning and it served as a gentle daily reminder. In the evening, I would review the **Today** column and plan my actions for the next day. The advantage of doing this in the evening is that you are already tired, making it more likely you'll plan realistically for the coming day. At least that's how it worked for me. In the morning when starting up, I am way more ambitious and enthusiastic than when I am longing for my bed.

On Sunday evenings, I focused on the **This week** column and what needed planning for that coming week. On the last day of the month, I worked on the column **This month** to see which actions were needed for the coming month.

Overall, I was very pleased with this physical board. It feels very gratifying to move sticky notes to **Done**. Also, due to limited space on the board, you protect yourself from stuffing too many sticky notes in one column.

When we moved house, I did not have such a convenient space on the wall. So, I switched to a digital Journey Planner (Trello in my case, but there are many other apps out there). It is more convenient because now I have my Journey Planner with me all the time. I can inspect it anywhere, anytime. When I have a new idea or remember something important, I can add it to my digital Journey Planner immediately. I started using it for my work planning as well as for bigger personal projects like renovating the garden or writing and publishing this book.

I noticed one caveat with a digital planning app on my phone. Because I use all kinds of different apps, it was quite easy to overlook my Journey Planner, even when it was located on the home screen. So, there's still room for improvement!

Looking back now, I found it inspiring to stand at my physical board and have an oversight on the overall plan. I might switch back to a physical board again once I figure out a good spot to put it.

Summary

In this chapter, you learned how to transform the goals from your Steering Wheel into actionable planning. Your personal Journey Planner visualizes the actions needed to reach your goals, just like a Scrum board used by Scrum teams. The Journey Planner supports your journey towards happiness as it helps you stay focused and loyal to your goals despite the circumstances.

To use your Journey Planner effectively:

- Set up a task board with columns Goals, To do, This month, This week, Today, and Done.

- Define actions clearly and concisely.

- Break actions down so they can be completed in a day.

- Adopt daily, weekly, and monthly habits to execute your planned actions and update your Journey Planner as you go.

You can make a physical task board, as introduced in this chapter. You can also use a planning app on your phone or put everything in a spreadsheet. Whatever works for you. Experiment with different systems and keep looking for new ways to improve. The best task management system is the one you'll use, because then you stand a much better chance to stay loyal to your goals and reach happiness.

Because time is often limited and we quickly overestimate how much we can achieve, choosing which actions to pick up first and which can come later is wise. That is why we will look at various ways to prioritize your actions in the next chapter so your planning becomes more realistic when working towards your goals.

You can't save time.
You can only spend it
differently.

- Unknown

Mapping your priorities

When we had just moved into our current house there was some DIY work to do. The interior design was outdated, and we wanted to upgrade the living room, bathroom, and bedrooms. At the same time, I had set goals on personal health, publishing Scrumpy Dad stories on Medium, spending quality time with our kids and family, as well as contributing to charity work. I noticed some stress building up as I realized that I would not be able to fulfil all my roles successfully, and so my happiness dropped.

To get some clarity for myself, I created an exercise to assess how much I needed and wanted to invest in these different roles. The exercise helped me to prioritize on my roles. I decided to pause my role as a writer and charity volunteer. I also reduced my social activities. Making these deliberate choices made it easier for me to focus on the DIY projects. In fact, accepting the fact that I temporarily limited my time in some roles allowed me to enjoy the DIY work and feel happy without regret.

In the previous chapter, I mentioned the importance of prioritizing your actions but not how. We will cover that here. Prioritization is crucial because our time and energy are limited, and doing everything at once will not work. It just keeps you busy running around while your frustration increases and your motivation decreases. When you know how to prioritize, you can make well-founded decisions about what to pick up first and what to pick up later. That will dramatically increase your chances of achieving your goals and make you feel proud and happy.

Prioritizing creates focus because you say yes to one thing and no to many other things. When you can focus on a single task, you have a higher chance of finishing it. Multi-tasking sounds impressive, but people forget about the waste of task-switching. Research shows that task-switching causes a lot of energy and drains the brain[6]. You avoid this energy loss by focusing on a single task at a time.

There are various ways to prioritize. In this chapter we will cover the following techniques:

- **Eisenhower matrix**
- **Effort vs. Impact**
- **Roles-on-the-Radar**
- **Focus & control**

Let's see in more detail how these methods work in practice. Feel free to experiment so you can choose the method that works for you, depending on the situation.

Eisenhower matrix

This one is a classic. This prioritization method is named after Dwight D. Eisenhower, the 34th president of the United States. This technique is often used for time management purposes and works effectively.

The basic idea is to classify all your actions according to two criteria:

- **Urgency**: how urgent is this action? Is it time-critical? Is there a deadline coming up? Or is timing less of an issue?
- **Importance**: how vital is this action for you? Is it critical for your goals or purpose? Does it matter to you? Or don't you care too much about this action?

Instructions

First, get yourself a large sheet of paper, at least A3, or 2 sheets of A4 stuck together. You can also put 4 A4 sheets together for an even larger working space if you want. Draw a 2x2 matrix. The horizontal axis defines importance from low to high. The vertical axis represents urgency, also from low to high.

> **TIP**
>
> *As an alternative to a big sheet of paper, you can also use a wall, a door, the side of a cupboard, a tabletop, or any other surface. You can use tape to create the matrix or just the axes.*

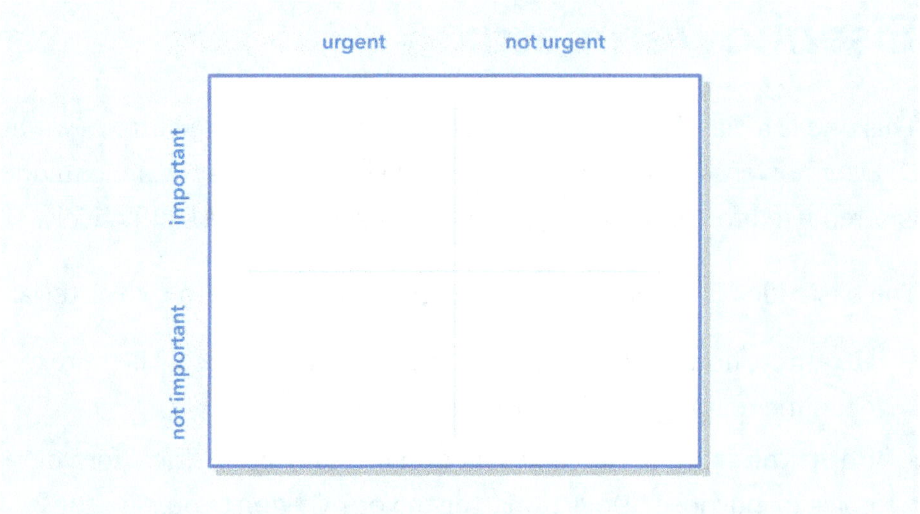

Eisenhower matrix template.

Write the items you want to prioritize on sticky notes. It might be all the actions on your Journey Planner, or maybe all actions related to one of your personal goals. The big benefit of using sticky notes in this exercise is that you can still move them around when you have new insights and want to change your mind.

Now, put all your sticky notes on the matrix based on their relative urgency and importance. Based on your classification, your actions fall in either one of four quadrants, where each quadrant indicates how to deal with the corresponding actions.

Do: urgent and important

These actions are time critical and important to you. There could be significant consequences if you fail to complete these actions in a timely fashion. So, you better get started on these and get them done. These actions are typically in your **Today** or **This week** column of your Journey Planner.

Decide: not urgent but important

These actions matter to you, but there is no time pressure (yet). Because the actions in this quadrant are not urgent, you can afford to plan these for next week or next month, so make sure to put them on your Journey Planner. The challenge will be to execute on your planning and stay loyal to your goals.

You should be attentive to this category of actions because we tend to focus only on urgent actions, even if they are less important. These actions can become urgent over time when you ignore them for too long. So, learn to plan ahead to steer more proactively on important items and get less manipulated by urgency alone.

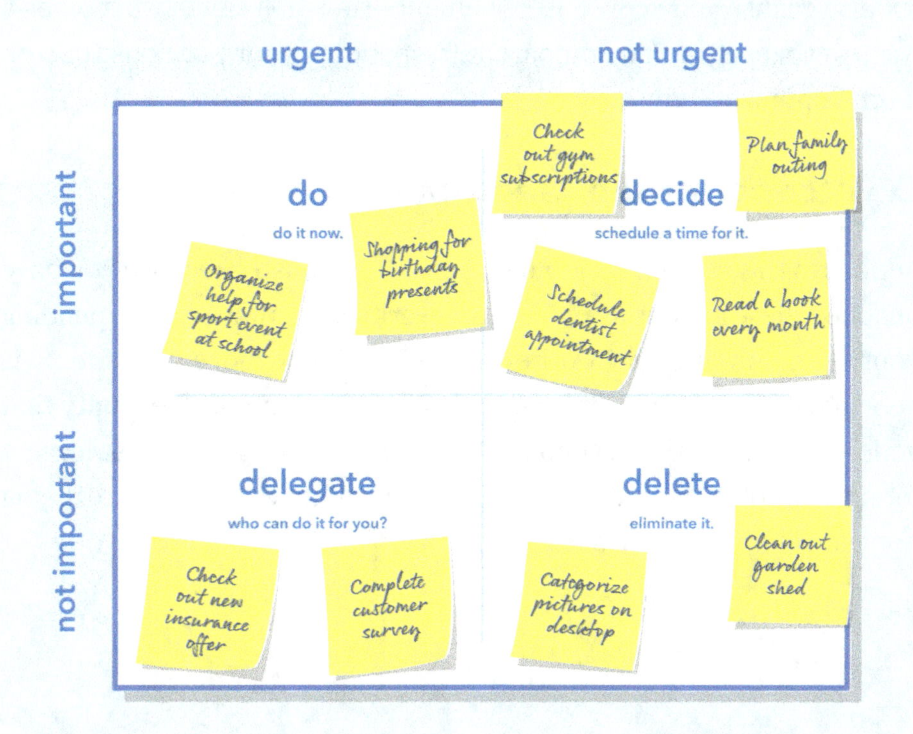

Example of a completed Eisenhower matrix.

Delegate: urgent but not important

These actions are time-critical but not crucial to you. Conventional time management wisdom suggests delegating these actions. Yet, from a Scrum Master perspective, I wouldn't consider involving others to carry out actions I don't care about. If it's not essential to me, why bother others, right?

Many interrupts typically fall into this category. Although you cannot plan interruptions (they happen), you can prepare by minimizing the chance of being interrupted and by deciding how to respond when it happens.

If you still choose to pick up such an action, aim to reduce the time spent. Because you scored it low on importance, it quickly becomes a waste, especially if you compare it to spending your precious time on more important items.

Delete: not urgent and not important

Actions in this category should be considered waste. Because you have qualified these actions as neither time-critical nor important, spending your time and energy in other quadrants is far more valuable. It is good advice to willfully embrace that choice and not to feel guilty that actions in this quadrant keep lingering on collecting dust. Just leave it for now; it's okay. Or even better, delete these actions if you dare. Being honest will bring you peace of mind.

Effort vs. Impact

The Effort vs. Impact method initially looks similar to the Eisenhower matrix and has a more business-like approach. It will help you to decide if a particular action is worth the effort based on the expected impact, also known as the expected Return on Investment (ROI). In other words: do you think it is worth it?

The basic idea here is that you relatively order your actions according to two criteria:

- **Effort**: how much time or energy will it take to complete this action?
- **Impact**: how does this action contribute to reaching your goals? Does it support you in living your purpose and values?

Instructions

First, get yourself a large sheet of paper, at least A3, or 2 sheets of A4 stuck together. You can also put 4 A4 sheets together for an even larger working space. Draw a 2x2 matrix. The horizontal axis shows the expected effort from low to high. The vertical axis shows the expected impact, also from low to high.

Bring enough sticky notes to write down all the items you want to prioritize. It might be all the actions on your Journey Planner, or maybe all actions are related to one of your goals or personal projects. It is up to you to select actions that need prioritizing.

Now, place all your sticky notes on the matrix based on their relative expected effort and expected impact. This classification exercise is not about being perfectly right where you put sticky notes on the chart. It is more about the relative ordering of action items to each other. This is even more true because you do not always know upfront how much effort a specific action will require or how big or small the impact will be. So, let's not waste too much time on being perfectly right.

Take a look at your Steering Wheel and check what is on there, in particular, what you have listed in the Goals, Values and Purpose sections. This serves as your context to decide on the impact of actions. Actions that contribute to your goals, values or purpose have a higher impact than those that contribute less.

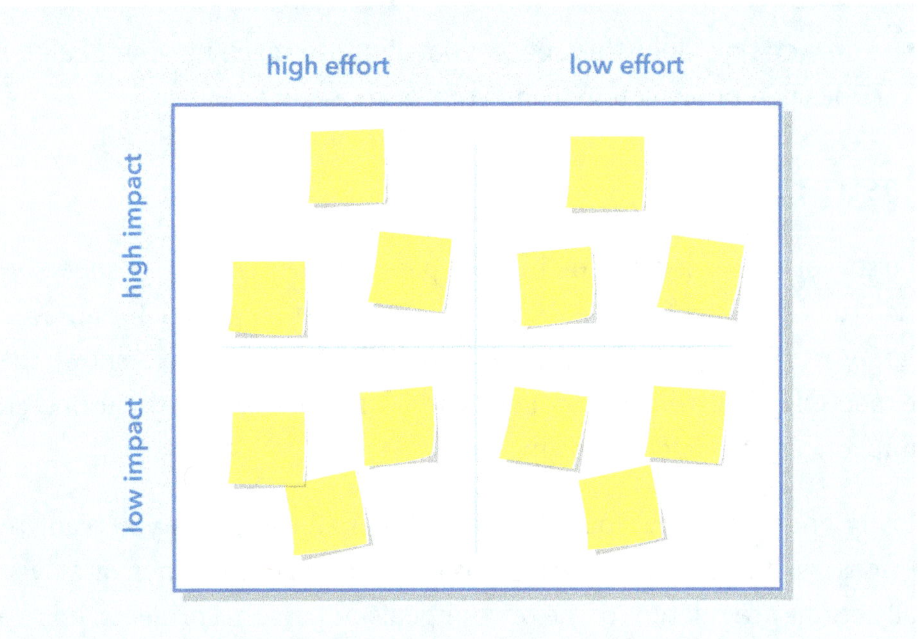

Effort vs. Impact matrix.

Based on your classification, your actions fall into one of four quadrants, where each quadrant indicates how to deal with the corresponding actions.

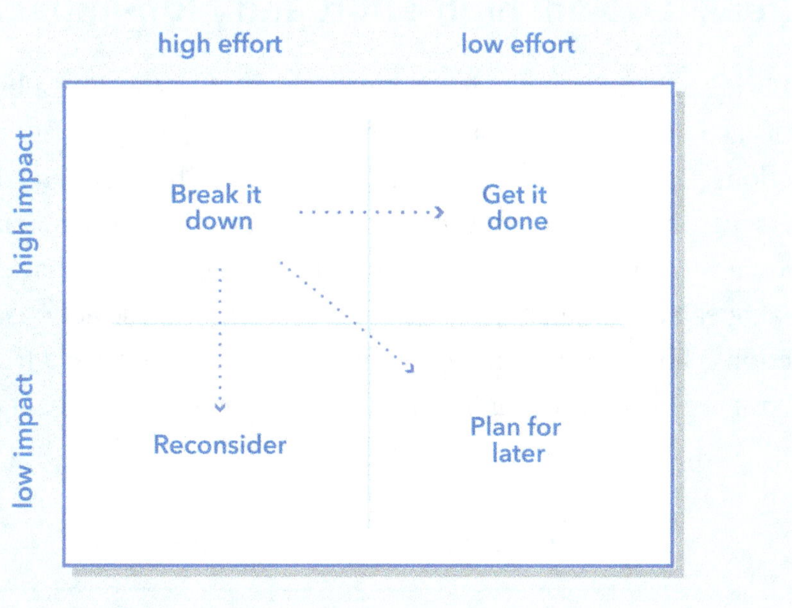

Effort vs. Impact matrix: actions for each quadrant.

Get it done: low-effort and high-impact

Action items in this quadrant qualify as low-hanging fruit or quick wins. Because you expect a high impact with little effort, it is worth getting these items done in the short term. You typically put these actions in your Journey Planner for **Today** or **This week**.

Plan for later: low-effort and low-impact

These actions are relatively easy to complete, but they also contribute little to your goals, values or purpose. When you are running out of high-impact actions, it is time to look at these actions and decide if they are worth picking up. You could plan them for later, so put them in the **To do** column of your Journey Planner.

Break it down: high-effort and high-impact

This is an intriguing quadrant because you are expecting a big impact but also anticipating a large investment in time or energy for these actions. So, the actual ROI might still be low. These actions deserve a closer look to figure out if they can be broken down further. In Scrum, we call this refinement: splitting into smaller pieces that are more manageable and valuable. When breaking down these actions, the new actions can end up in any of the other quadrants. Proceed from there. If you are lucky, you will find some low-effort & high-impact actions.

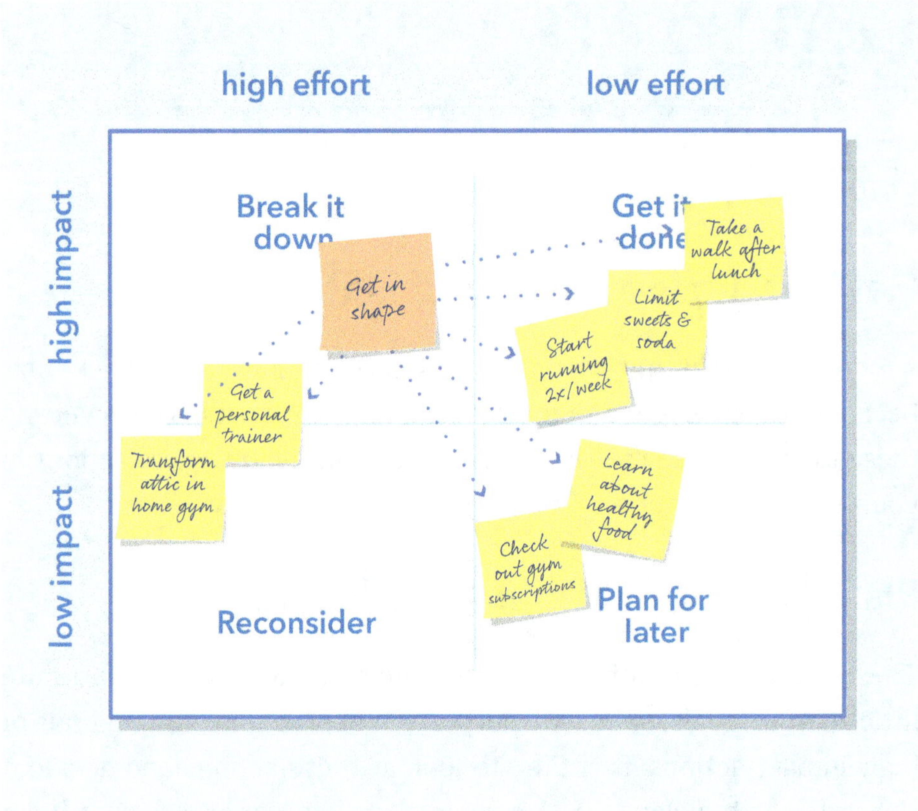

Example of an action broken down.

Reconsider: high-effort and low-impact

Actions that cost you plenty of time and energy but contribute little to your goals, values or purpose should be handled carefully. These actions are expected to have a low ROI. Since we are prioritizing, these actions can wait and maybe should be dropped altogether.

Roles-on-the-Radar

Do you ever feel frustrated about everything you want to do, knowing there won't be enough time to complete it? Or, while you dedicate your precious time to one aspect of your life, you get that nagging feeling you're neglecting another more important area? You fulfill various roles in your life, and these roles will be competing for your precious time. I developed a simple tool called Roles-on-the-Radar; it can help you choose where to invest your limited time and energy and which role(s) to focus on.

Instructions

Your roles, as listed on your Steering Wheel, come in handy here. Take a sheet of A4 paper and draw a radar chart. Ensure you have as many axes as the number of roles you identified. Write your roles at the end of the axes, one role per axis.

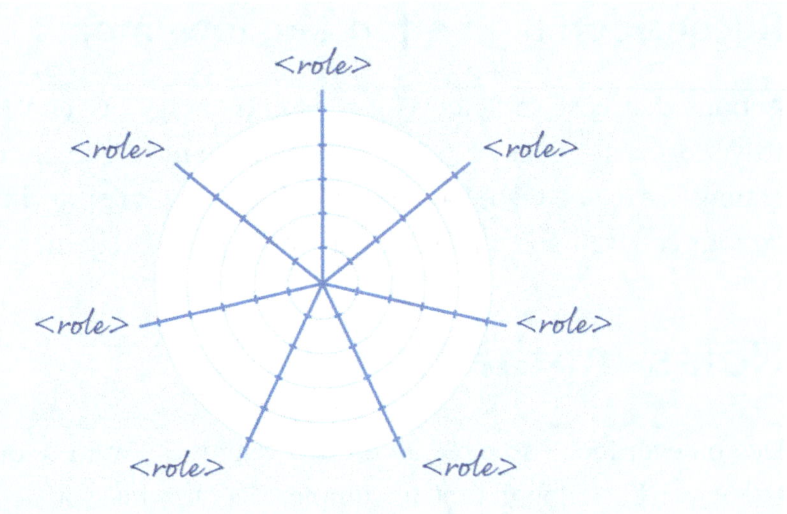

Roles-on-the-Radar chart template.

How it works:

1. Score your happiness in each of your roles. This is a relative score. You mark the far end of an axis if everything is going perfectly for you. If you are extremely unhappy about your performance in this role, you put a mark near the center of the chart. If it's 50/50, you put a mark halfway through the axis. You get the idea. Complete the radar chart for all your roles. Be honest to yourself without judgment to get the most out of this exercise.

2. Connect the marks on the axes.

3. Fill the inner area of the radar chart.

4. The filled area symbolizes your achievements in each role so far. You'll notice that you are doing quite well in some roles. Take a moment to take credit for that. We often forget to acknowledge ourselves for what we have achieved.

5. Examine the unfilled outer area of the radar chart. This represents your potential. Roles will stand out where you think there is room

for improvement. Decide which roles to focus on to make the next step. This will depend very much on your personal situation and the roles you feel the greatest urgency to invest in.

6. For each of these selected roles, check for related goals and actions on your Journey Planner. If they are not specified yet, you first need to define new actions and add them to make your investment actionable.

7. Now, you can rearrange the goals and actions on your Journey Planner based on the newly prioritized roles.

With the Roles-on-the-Radar exercise, you'll know you're focusing on the right things. Refer to the chapter 'Planning your journey' for more practical advice on planning goals and actions.

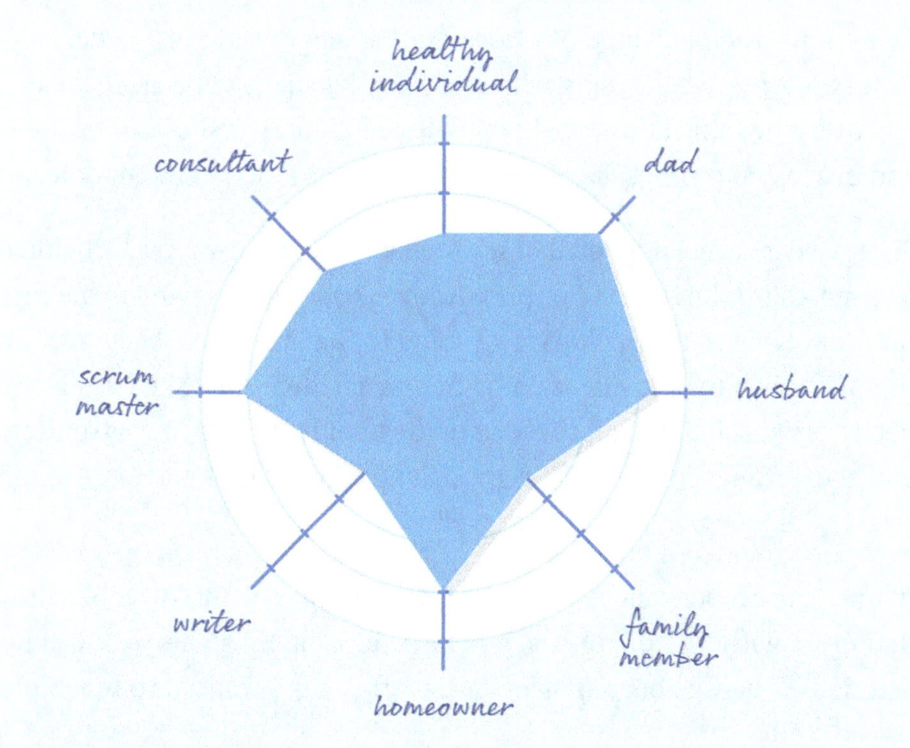

Example of a completed Roles-on-the-Radar chart.

Focus & control

Sometimes the challenge of prioritizing is bigger than just ordering a list of options and choosing which one to pick up first, because life can feel overwhelming at times. When you no longer oversee your options, and every choice feels like a trap, you may feel stuck in the middle.

Several years ago, I noticed that my teenage daughter was overwhelmed by everything she had on her plate: moving out on her own for the first time, applying to internships, searching for a part-time job, staying on top of her health, and maintaining her social life. While she has always been very disciplined, all these activities competed for her attention, and she struggled to find the right balance. She wasn't getting enough sleep, which began to affect her wellbeing.

It hurt me to see one of my kids struggling. I wanted to help my daughter without telling her what to do (not that she would have listened – she was becoming an adult, after all). I wanted to teach her how to manage multiple tasks, a skill she would need for the rest of her life.

In my job as a Scrum Master, I guide teams in understanding their priorities so they can find focus. I thought about all the exercises and interventions I've used in my work and eventually landed on one that could help my daughter sort out her scattered thoughts: the WADE Matrix[7]. WADE stands for What, Analog, Digital, and Execute. It's also the name of its creator, Scrum Master Derek Wade. The WADE Matrix is a visual tool that lets you see everything on your mind and helps identify where you should focus your time and energy. If you're feeling overwhelmed, it can reveal the steps you should take to get back to clarity.

My daughter has become somewhat used to her Scrumpy Dad bringing Agile & Scrum techniques home, so she was open to trying this exercise when I told her about it. I grabbed a pen and a stack of sticky notes. I was looking for some wall space to work on and settled for the large cupboard in our living room.

What: gather data

To begin, I asked my daughter to write down everything she had going on in her life – one item per sticky note. This was an excellent way for her to empty her head. She jotted down things like: "going to the gym," "quitting her current job," "looking for a new job", and "finding a boyfriend." The result was an impressive cloud of sticky notes on the cupboard.

Analog: use relative weighting

Next, on the left side of the cupboard, I created a vertical axis —
essentially, a straight line with arrows on each side. At the bottom of
the axis, I wrote "going well," and at the top, "going badly." (Note: You
can write "not going so well" if you prefer, but I'm Dutch and therefore
blunt by design.)

I asked my daughter to arrange her sticky notes vertically based on
these two opposites. Things in her life that were going well should be
placed at the bottom, while things that were going poorly should be
situated at the top. Everything else could go somewhere in between.
She didn't have to create a perfect representation of her life — I simply
wanted her to see where the items sat relative to one another. In my
job, this process is called relative weighting, and it helps people make
better decisions.

Next, I created a horizontal axis at the bottom of the cupboard. On
the left, I wrote "can control," on the right, I wrote "can't control." I
then told my daughter to align the sticky notes horizontally based on
her control over the issues. Each sticky note's vertical position was
to remain unchanged during this exercise. After moving the first
few sticky notes to the left, my daughter started to realize what was
happening. "I see," she mumbled. "What's on the left are things I can
take care of myself."

Digital: categorize

When my daughter was done, I divided the area into a 2x2 grid. I then
categorized the four quadrants, as shown in the diagram. Now it was
time for the final step.

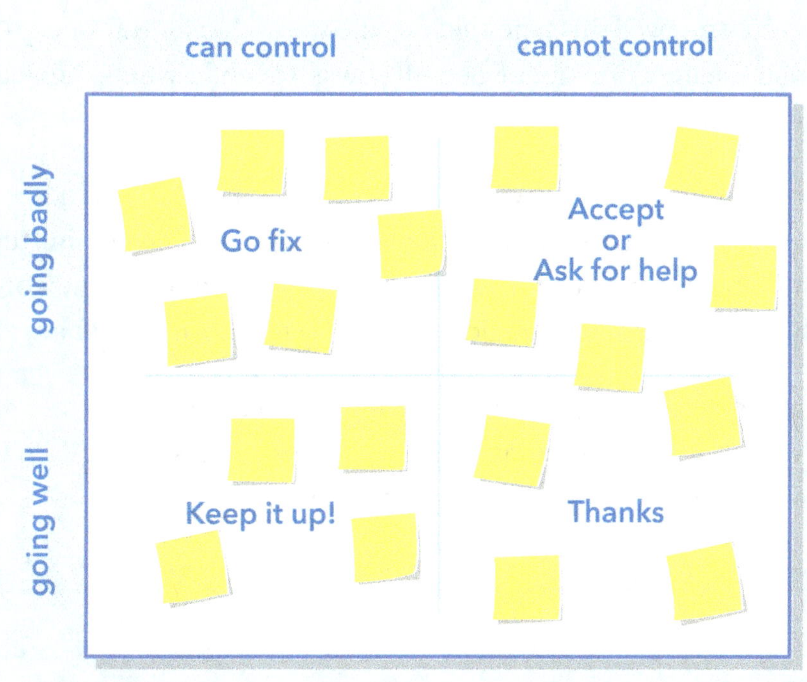

The WADE matrix and the four categories.

Execute: take action

Looking at the chart, my daughter immediately relaxed. She understood what the quadrants meant. The **Go fix**-quadrant was filled with what she should devote her time and energy to. There weren't many items in that quadrant compared to the number of anxieties swirling through her mind at the beginning of the exercise. This settled her quite a bit.

Next, we looked at the **Accept or Ask for help** quadrant, filled with things going poorly and outside her control. She had to decide for each item: She could either accept the reality of it and let it go or seek help. One sticky note in that quadrant contained her worry about what other people thought of her. A burden seemed to lift when she realized she had no control over this. She told me she wanted to let this one go and focus on feeling good about herself. I was touched when she shared this revelation with me.

The lower two quadrants were filled with things going well in her life. It was good for her to see how much was working. She committed to keeping up her routines for the areas in which she had some control (like her friendships). She could feel grateful for those out of her reach.

As a father, I was happy to see my daughter relaxed again. It's freeing to view your mind's contents right before you. You can see what's in your hands and, even more powerfully, what isn't.

Summary

In this chapter, you have learned the ropes of prioritizing. Prioritizing creates clarity and focus on the most valuable tasks, which you can apply to your Journey Planner. It helps you decide where to invest your time and energy to reach those goals that bring you closer to happiness.

The prioritizing techniques covered in this chapter are:

- **Eisenhower matrix**
- **Effort vs. Impact**
- **Roles-on-the-Radar**
- **Focus & control**

Feel free to experiment and pick the technique that appeals most to you when prioritizing at a particular moment. You will find that some techniques are more suited for some situations than others. Now that you have seen a few different techniques, you have a set to choose from to vary your approach. Ultimately, it's not so relevant that you have all your actions in a perfectly ordered list. As long as it's clear which actions are your top 5 or top 10, you know where to focus and which ones to ignore for now.

Planning and prioritizing are all very nice and helpful, but when we start executing plans, reality hits. Only some things will go as planned, other actions work out differently than expected, and unexpected situations will arise. Therefore, we will look at practical ways to deal with these new insights and experiences. The next chapter is about checking your course towards your goals and how you are doing on your journey towards happiness.

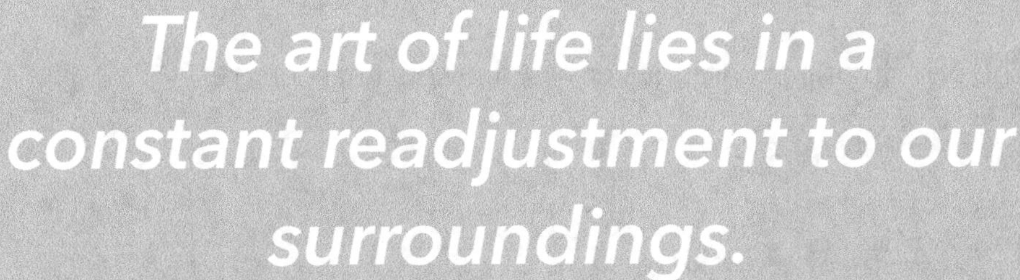

The art of life lies in a constant readjustment to our surroundings.

- Kakuzo Okakura

Checking your course

For my personal development, I have scheduled a weekly appointment with myself on Sunday mornings to reflect on how I'm doing. Making it a recurring routine, it has become such a comfortable habit that I can't even remember when I started it. I take out a notebook and pen and start writing. It helps to get it all out of my head, and it is easier to keep oversight when you can read stuff back if you want.

The exercise basically boils down to investigating what is going well and what I'd like to improve on next week. Writing down what is going well provides me with instant gratitude, because it's easy to forget good moments and successes, just by taking things for granted. By looking at improvements for the coming week I hold myself accountable for my personal growth. By keeping these improvements simple and achievable, I feel empowered to follow up on them successfully. Once achieved, that's another boost for my happiness.

In this chapter, you'll learn how to apply this inspection and adaptation routine for yourself. That may seem weird initially because we are not used to a routine of checking the course of our personal journeys. It might take a significant life event like illness, a broken relationship, the loss of a job, or the death of somebody dear before we consider checking in with ourselves.

Just imagine you have left the harbor and are now sailing on the open sea, heading towards your next destination. With the steering wheel firmly in your hands, you check the plan you made for this part of the journey. But checking the plan is not enough. You must also check your environment to make sense of your current situation. Which way are those dark clouds moving? Did the wind turn? Do you still have enough food and water on board?

You must regularly check how your journey is progressing and if you are still on course. If you are, that's great and a reassuring confirmation. If not, you have two options: adjust your course or your destination.

The power of retrospectives

As a Scrum Master, part of my job is to help teams improve how they work and collaborate over time. One way I do this is through something called a Sprint Retrospective. Scrum teams plan their work in short, iterative timeframes, typically 2-4 weeks long. At the end of every Sprint, a team will evaluate their performance, figuring out what went well and what can be improved.

A Sprint Retrospective is a powerful event allowing team members to make sense of their most recent experiences. They can celebrate wins, acknowledge setbacks, recognize patterns, and create plans for improvement based on new insights. It is quite common to identify three steps in a Sprint Retrospective:

- **Collect data**: to share the available information about the past sprint.

- **Generate insights**: to identify patterns and collect lessons learnt.

- **Decide what to do**: come up with actionable improvements.

One classic retrospective format is the sailing boat retrospective. The starting point for this retrospective is a drawing of a sailing boat out at sea, which symbolizes the participants on their journey together. The island represents their common goal or purpose. The wind symbolizes forces that propel them forward, whereas the anchor stands for anything that is slowing them down. The reef depicts the risks that are lurking underwater. By collecting information and creating insights on these various elements, the participants create a shared understanding of their current situation. Based on these new gained insights they can figure out how to navigate from there.

Sailing boat retrospective template.

The personal retrospective

To know how you are doing while working towards your personal goals, it is essential to measure your progress somehow. To take the next step toward your goal, you need to know where you are now. You need to do this regularly, like every week or month, to keep making adjustments when needed and stay on course.

Measuring progress

Metrics are all around us in our everyday life. Current time, today's temperature, the battery charge level of your devices (including electric car, e-bike etc.), your expected time of arrival, the balance of your bank account, the number of likes on your latest social media post, and many more. Most are helpful because they provide insight and help you make decisions.

I have been experimenting a lot with finding relevant metrics that support how I am doing. It seemed a bit artificial at first, but I learned how it can help in adapting my behavior and placing focus on what matters to me. Here are some examples of my personal metrics.

Metrics for my goal to stay fit

One of my most important goals is my health: I want to feel strong and healthy every day, mentally and physically, so I can grow old and stay in good shape.

- I found it challenging to drink enough water during the day. So, I installed a simple counter app on my phone to tick off every glass of water I consumed. Seeing this number on my phone's home screen every time I glanced at it reminded me to refill my glass.

- I have been tracking my weight in a spreadsheet and later with a smart scale and an app to lose some kilos. Weight is a lagging indicator; it confronts you with yesterday's choices. It only helps a little in controlling what you want it to be. So, I subscribed to a lifestyle program to try something else for a change (I use Noom now, but there are plenty of alternatives). The app supports me in tracking my weight but also in logging consumed food and burned calories. Now, I have a good insight into my daily calorie budget to make healthier daily choices.

- Every day, I want to get some basic exercise. I have a weekly checklist in my planner app to tick off every day I do yoga, cycling, running, or walking. When my schedule is tight, I take the stairs to the 10th floor at work as an alternative workout; that counts, too, for me.

All these measurements support me in making more conscious decisions to take good care of my health. It also triggers me to get creative when things are not working out as planned.

Metrics for my goal to get better at golf

My partner and I started playing golf two years ago. I really love this game because it is an intriguing mix of technical skill and mind control. Plus, I get to spend time outdoors for a few hours! I practice or play a course every week to improve myself as an amateur golfer. I keep notes to see how I am doing:

- Holes played equal or better as expected with my handicap
- Holes scored par (equal as expected for a pro)
- Golf balls lost (risk of the game)
- Golf balls in bunker
- Situations that went well (putting, hitting out of a bunker)

- Situations that I want to improve (keeping my cool when teeing off on the first hole with people watching)

Keeping these statistics helps me evaluate my play, acknowledge where it is going well, and help me focus on what to practice more next time (instead of just completing a standard routine).

Metrics for my book project

For the project of creating this book, A Scrum Master's Guide to Happiness, I have been using metrics, too. I was blessed with a small team of reviewers to get feedback on my writing. I sent them chapters for review and a short survey to solicit their opinion on particular topics. Apart from open questions, I also asked them to rate chapter titles, quotes, and other manuscript parts on a scale of 1-5. These scores helped me assess the quality of my writing and allowed me to improve it where needed.

Weekly retrospective routine

For my personal development, I have scheduled a weekly appointment with myself on Sunday mornings, which works well. You will need to find the time and frequency that works best for you. Of course, you can carry out a personal retrospective as a mental exercise, reflecting on last week in your head. I prefer using pen and paper to write everything down. It helps to get it all out of my head and it is easier to keep oversight when you can read stuff back.

For my weekly retrospectives, like Sprint Retrospectives, there are plenty of methods and formats to choose from. One of my favorite formats is called "Three Ls." The Ls stand for Liked, Learned, and

Lacked. All you have to do is ask yourself three questions: What did I like? What did I learn? What was lacking?

Inspection

Draw four columns on a sheet of A4 paper or in a notebook. In the left column, list your roles, like parent, neighbor, runner, and friend. When I do this exercise, I also include "healthy me," as taking care of my body and mind is one of my biggest priorities.

In the remaining three columns, write Liked, Learned, and Lacked. This is where the real work happens.

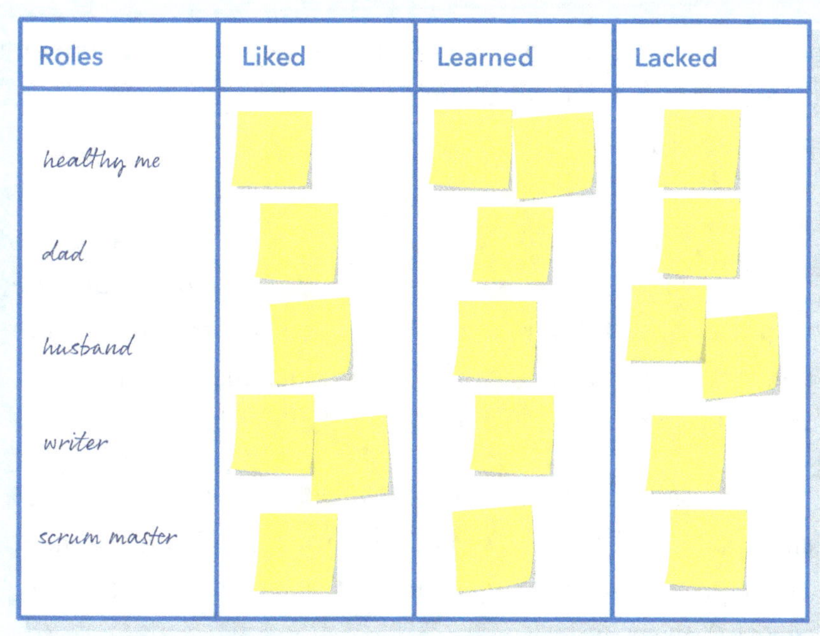

Liked/Learned/Lacked retrospective template.

Retrospectives provide an opportunity for the process that Scrum Masters call inspection and adaptation. So first, inspect how you're doing by filling in the three columns:

Liked: What were your wins of the week? Note your successes, big or small.

Learned: What were your discoveries? Here, you can start to notice patterns.

Lacked: What could have gone better? This is where you clarify your disappointments and frustrations. In writing them out, you often uncover your subconscious expectations. You begin to see how you might be setting yourself up for failure.

Fill out the sheet in any order that makes sense to you. Pinpointing what I learned is the most challenging column, so I start there and then complete the other two.

> **Liked**: *Now that my kids are grown and have moved out, I see them less, which I don't love. However, I like that we stay in touch through social media, which allows us to continue to interact in a fun way. I want to keep that a priority.*
>
> **Learned**: *I learned that weekends are tricky to lose weight. I enjoy wine and tapas. I should take it easy – I can still have my favorite foods, but I will eat smaller portions more slowly, savoring every bite.*

Lacked: I spent hardly any time writing my book last week. I need to structure my days differently since I want to prepare it for review in a few months. I will change my mode of transportation from motorbike to train so I can write during my commute.

Adaptation

Based on what I've written, I adapt by choosing 1-2 concrete actions I want to pursue in the coming week and then adding them to my Journey Planner. If I do them well, I should see the impact of these improvements in next week's retrospective.

> **TIP**
>
> *Experiment by formulating your improvement actions as if/then rules: If <some event occurs> then <I do this>. Our brains are sensitive to this kind of programming.*

The Three Ls format is simple and effective. If you want to try something else, plenty of other retrospective formats are available. I have included some great resources for these formats in the chapter 'Inspiration'. Just experiment and find out what works for you.

Monthly retrospective routine

After conducting my weekly retrospectives for a year, I was very focused on just the weekly stuff, not seeing bigger patterns. I started doing monthly retrospectives and eventually even yearly retrospectives.

These sessions help you take a step back and see larger patterns, which you might miss when only reviewing weekly.

I take a slightly different approach for these monthly sessions because I want to look at my progress over the year. I still evaluate how I am doing in my roles but also inspect the year goals I've set for myself.

Inspection

I typically start off by rating myself for each role and goal. That is an easy start to see how I view my performance so far. A very simple way is to assign a score on a scale from 1 to 10. If you like a more visual approach, you can also plot your scores on a radar plot (similar to the Roles-on-the-Radar exercise).

Next, I choose a retrospective format that seems right for the situation. Last month I used More/Keep/Less/Stop as a format which worked really nice:

More: what should I do more? Or maybe even start because it's important?

Keep: which activities should I continue? What works fine and is worth repeating?

Less: what activities should I reduce? What is costing too much time? Where is the waste?

Stop: which activities should I really stop doing? What is no longer needed or doesn't serve me?

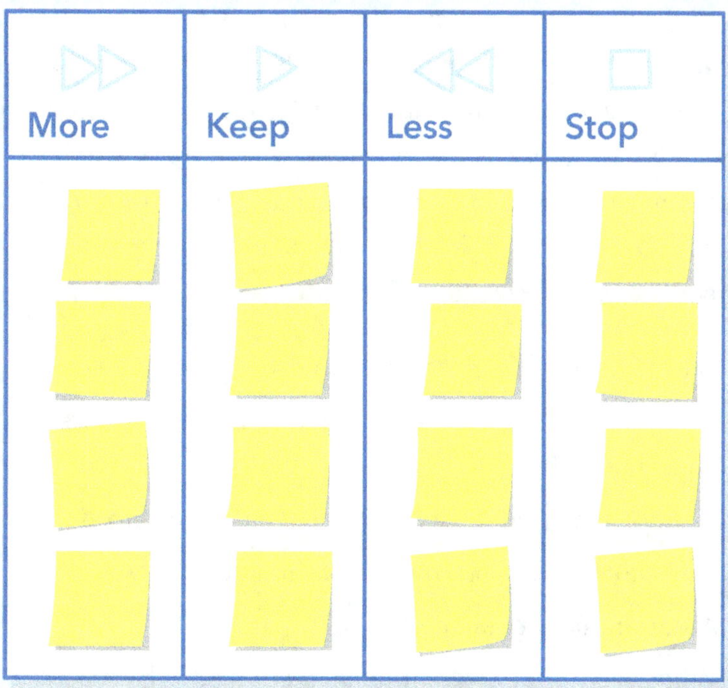

More/Keep/Less/Stop retrospective template.

Of course, you can carry out your retrospectives all on your own, but for some roles and goals, you most likely interact with others. How about asking them for input on how you are doing? Like in Scrum, you need to involve your stakeholders.

It's all great of course that I think I'm doing fine as a husband and a dad. But do my partner and kids agree on that? So, every now and again, typically when my partner and I are enjoying a walk along the river at the weekend, I bring up this topic. First, I share with her my latest insights and personal improvement actions. Just asking for feedback is typically too vague to answer. Instead, I ask her questions like:

- Is there anything that you dislike in my behavior?
- Are you content with how we are taking care of the household jobs?
- Is there anything I can do different to make your life easier?
- Do I show my affection for you enough?
- Are we having enough fun?
- What are our strong points as a couple? What could make it even better?
- What are you looking forward to?

My kids are now in their early twenties and living their own lives. Of course, I am still their dad, so I want to support them whenever that is needed. Here are some example questions that I have asked my kids to check in with them:

- Do you like how we stay in touch by phone and social media?
- Do I show enough interest in what's going on in your life?
- Do you enjoy visiting our place?
- Do you feel you can tell or ask me anything?
- Is there anything I can still do to be a better dad?

Adaptation

Based on the insights so far, I start generating improvement actions. They often start bubbling up during the previous step, so I write them down for later. To be realistic, I choose only a few improvement actions that I want to follow up on and include on my Journey Planner. You can always go back later for more ideas (but experience shows that hardly ever happens).

Since choosing is often hard, I typically ask myself which of these improvement actions are the biggest small step towards my goals. The biggest small step refers to the smallest effort that could lead to the biggest result. Keeping it small helps to start and get it done. If improvement actions are too big, you will feel overwhelmed and less motivated to make it happen. Of course, there is never a 100% guarantee that an improvement will yield the intended result, but you should at least feel optimistic about it.

Another approach to picking the best possible improvement actions is to apply one of the prioritization techniques from the chapter 'Mapping your priorities'.

What I particularly like about the More/Keep/Less/Stop format is that it highlights a need for balance. Often, I'm quite ambitious and want to start up new initiatives or intensify a certain hobby, but if there is nothing that I will do less or even stop, how will I find the time to make this happen? So, it helps to stay realistic and make conscious choices.

Yearly retrospective routine

Weeks and months may fly by, but the start of a new year doesn't go unnoticed. It is also the time for new year's resolutions, which never last long as we all know. I think that one of the reasons is that we are tempted to look forward to the new year without learning from the past year. That's why I consider the end of the year a great moment to reflect and contemplate on plans for the new year to set ourselves up for success. As such, reviewing last year helps to set better goals this year. By taking into account the lessons from last year, we improve our chances of reaching our goals in the new year in our pursuit for happiness.

Like me, you may find out that it's quite hard to remember all the highs and lows of an entire year. Here are a few tips to get you started:

- Browse through the photo gallery on your mobile phone or computer. This is a great opportunity to relive the past year one more time, and can be a profound experience. Lots of good stuff to be grateful for.
- Browse through your agenda. You will find all kinds of events, appointments, dates, ceremonies and parties that you attended last year.
- Do you keep a diary or journal? That's another valuable source of information on what kept you busy over the past year.
- If you have been doing monthly retrospectives, you can refer to these as well.

While you are browsing through last year and reliving past memories, make a list of all the major events that summarize that year for you.

The main purpose of this step is refreshing your memory about the year gone by.

Inspection

Let's start with all your roles as listed in your Steering Wheel:

- How do you assess yourself on your roles? The simplest way is to rate yourself on a 1-10 scale or a 1–5-star rating. If you prefer a more visual approach, use the Roles-on-the-Radar exercise (chapter 'Mapping your priorities').
- What went well for each of the roles?
- What did you learn in your various roles?

This is a great way to capitalize on your insights on fulfilling your roles in life.

Next are all the goals that you had set for the past year, regardless of if they are done, still in progress, or maybe never started (or even canceled). All these goals carry valuable lessons.

For each goal on your Steering Wheel, write down the following:

- Did you manage to achieve your goal? Is it still work in progress? Is it still on your to-do list? Or maybe you even decided to drop it?
- What was the end result? What did you get out of it?
- What went well while working on this goal?
- What did you learn from working on this goal? Which new insights do you have now?

Next, take a step back and see if you can find any similarities or patterns in the results, the highlights, and the lessons for the goals and roles. What does this show you? Are new strengths surfacing? How can you exploit these insights and lessons in other areas of your life?

This is also an excellent moment to check out the other sections of your Steering Wheel to see if everything still accurate and relevant. You will start to see the bigger patterns in your life and what helped you to reach your goals and fulfill your roles. The main impact of this exercise is to get inspired by your successes and apply your new insights to your plans for the new year.

One of my ongoing goals is living healthy, both physically and mentally. These are some insights from my year retrospective:

- *I started yoga early mornings twice a week (energizing).*

- *Ran a few times on the weekend (luckily no knee problems).*

- *Weighed myself every day (discipline).*

- *Learned to enjoy doing totally nothing (pretty hard).*

- *Read more books (enlightening).*

- *Learned to play golf together with my partner (addictive).*

I also learned I was less fit than I always thought I was. Another insight was my eating behavior: to avoid throwing away food, I often choose to eat it instead. Not a healthy habit. But as I became aware of it, I could address this behavior by reducing portion sizes when preparing food and store away leftovers for next time.

Even though I didn't succeed in all my goals (I put writing a book about my divorce on hold), the insights were valuable and taught me some good lessons.

Adaptation

Based on your observations and insights from the previous step, you can now start preparing for the new year. Ask yourself:

- What should I keep that is still relevant for coming year?
- What should I drop because it is no longer relevant?
- What should I add because it becomes relevant in the coming year?

For example, it might be that some of your roles change due to changes in your personal situation or at work. Or, it may be that some unfinished goal is not so important to you anymore due to other priorities. That's all fine, do not cling on to items that are no longer important to you. Focus on what matters on your journey towards happiness. As a result, you will have an updated list of roles and goals that are important to you in the coming year.

Make sure that changes in roles and goals are reflected on your Steering Wheel and update the other sections where needed to keep it consistent and relevant. Please have a look at the chapter 'Steering towards happiness' for more detailed instructions. Update your Journey Planner with the new and updated goals and actions. Check out the chapter 'Planning your journey' for defining goals and planning realistically.

You may find that it takes about 2-3 hours looking back and planning for the new year. That might seem long at first, but please realize it's a one-time investment for a great new year. I always find it very energizing and inspiring to round up the year and prepare for the next one.

My family retrospective

Regularly checking course on your personal journey towards happiness is good advice. However, you can also use the retrospective practice as an intervention to tackle a tough situation, like I did once at home with my family. We need to travel back in time a little bit to when my kids were still teenagers.

During the week, my partner and I had the house to ourselves. On the weekends my daughter and son would come over, both teenagers and embracing puberty. Sometimes my partner's daughter also came over, and then it was really a full house. So yes, a mixed household with old and new family ties. As you can imagine, it was quite an adventure to build up a new family household.

From the start of our new relationship, my partner and I have been very much aware of this challenge. We have been making a big effort to make our new family setting work for everybody, which includes reading books[8] on parenting, talking to other parents in similar circumstances, and having deep late-night conversations to make sense of what happened during the day when we got into trouble. It takes plenty of love, patience, and understanding from everybody involved, especially from the parents. As a parent, I think you have a moral responsibility to make things work, for better and for worse.

The initial phase was a bit bumpy when everybody had to get used to each other and get to grips with the new situation. Spending time together in an amusement park is all quite well, and a fun way to get acquainted, but living together in an apartment and finding out about each other's peculiar habits and funny moods is something else. The simplest routines can become a surprise at best or a major annoyance at worst: where to put your wet towel after taking a shower, cleaning up in the kitchen, borrowing each other's stuff, where the laundry goes, etc.

Of course, we're all different individuals, each with their own values, principles, beliefs, and behavior. You could reason it's actually a miracle if it works out at all. Luckily, we found a way to live together that seemed to work out well. We learned how to communicate to keep the household going and have some fun along the way.

However, after a while, I felt we got stuck. As the linking pin between my teenage kids and my partner, I felt I had become the man in the middle, often liaising between both sides in case of misunderstandings or rising frustrations. It seemed to me that there was still room for improvement, to make all of us happier with less effort.

From idea to action

It so happens that in my work as Scrum Master, it's actually my main job to make teams work well together. I invest in creating a safe place to be open in communication and learn from experience, effectively deal with change, and adapt to new insights. My focus is always on continuous improvement and learning. So, I started wondering if and how I could put my work practices to good use at home. I quickly realized we should do a retrospective: looking back together, sharing insights, and identifying some improvement actions.

Homework

Experienced Scrum teams are comfortable running retrospectives as I explained earlier. They will grab some pens and sticky notes and start writing away, and then have a constructive discussion together. I couldn't see that happening with my family just yet, so I came up with some simple homework exercise so we'd all come to the kitchen table prepared.

I divided a piece of paper in three sections to address the following topics in three rounds:

- Which five values are most important to you in our family life together?
- What do you like about our family life?
- What would you like to change or try out?

For the first question, I had provided a set of value cards, to make it easier for them. I made a selection from a values card game that I bought for coaching sessions. There were a lot of values to choose from, some were more work related and so less suited for a family setting.

Some value cards that I selected were for example Fun, Openness, Freedom, Togetherness, Safety, etc. There were still plenty of values to choose from.

To test my plan, I decided to let my son go first. As a teenager who would spend hours gaming and sleeping, he'd be the least motivated to do this preparation exercise, I thought. I stopped by his room, a bit nervous to be honest, and explained to him what the purpose of the exercise was. He just nodded and told me he would give it a try later.

Quite relieved about this first small success I went downstairs and started filling out my own form. Much to my surprise, my son came downstairs within the hour, handing me over his form which he had fully completed! I was in total shock from his quick execution. He even mentioned it was quite fun to do. This looked very promising now! So, my daughter and partner were up next to do their homework too.

Actually, my partner was the most skeptical to hold this family retrospective. She feared the conversation could very well turn into a heated debate. And she was wondering if everybody would be able and willing to really open up to each other and hear each other's viewpoints. So, I took the time to explain my approach in a bit more detail to her, also emphasizing my experience as a Scrum Master to create a safe environment for all of us to talk freely. Luckily, she trusted me on this one.

The conversation

With all our busy schedules, it was a challenge to pick a free evening so we could have our pow-wow at the kitchen table, but 2 weeks later it was finally going to happen.

The first thing I noticed was the atmosphere in the room right before the session. We were cleaning up after dinner, everybody was getting ready and bringing their homework form. Already at that moment, I noticed a calm and peaceful mood settling in, as if everybody was tuning in to each other. And we hadn't even started...

Round 1: Values

In the opening round everybody got to talk about which values mattered most to them in our family setting. This was quite insightful because it was the first time we had talked so deeply about this. So, I learned that for my son, **Space** was an important value. He very much liked to be in his room, being left alone and having the freedom to play games, listen to music, doing homework, all at his own convenience. It helped me in letting go of my judgment that he was spending so much time on his own. He needed it and liked it!

When all of us had shared our most important values, we checked which values we had in common. There were only a few matches, so it was good to realize even more that we all had different needs.

Round 2: Keep what's good

The second round was nice too. It was very empowering to share what each of us liked in our family life, how we are organized and how we interact. It's also very rewarding as a parent to get some positive confirmation at times.

Round 3: Looking for improvements

The third round about suggestions for change was the most insightful. We took turns in discussing our ideas and suggestions. It was about very practical stuff (like more cooking together), but also about communication and engaging in conversations. I was very proud of my kids and how they participated in the conversation with my partner and me. Everybody was open to hearing each other out, asking questions, considering suggestions, and finding solutions that worked for all of us. There was no heated debate, just open conversations, increasing our mutual understanding.

The biggest surprise was for me. I had been very preoccupied with the preparation for this session and making sure everybody was doing fine, but I had forgotten that I was a participant too. Both of my kids had some feedback for me and suggestions on what I could do differently as their dad. No need to always check on school grades for instance, or less intervening if they have an argument. I was grateful they gave me such constructive feedback. I recognized what they meant and promised to change my behavior.

The outcome

Looking back, this family retrospective was a great way to invest in our family. Instead of only dealing with ad-hoc issues, we now invested in evaluating our complex family household together, talking about expectations, what went well, and what we wanted to improve. Setting the scene and providing some homework to prepare has been essential to making this work.

Since this family retrospective, everybody has experienced that our relationships have improved. There was more mutual understanding, and last but not least, we started talking about important stuff much more frequently. It became easier to address sensitive topics because we had experienced trust in our communication. I was very happy and proud of this outcome.

Summary

Life is hectic, and things will change, so you want to be able to deal with new information and insights. Evaluation is key to learning from your experiences. In this chapter, you have learned how to put the power of retrospectives to your personal use. We covered several retrospective formats like Liked/Learned/Lacked and More/Keep/Less/Stop.

In general, a retrospective consists of three steps:

- Collect data: to share the available information.
- Generate insights: to identify patterns and collect lessons learnt.
- Decide what to do: come up with actionable improvements.

Carrying out your personal retrospective every week helps you get into the self-reflection routine. Next, when you step back every month, and once a year, you allow yourself to take an even broader perspective. As a result, you will notice patterns that would go unnoticed otherwise, which helps you learn even more about yourself.

Take some time regularly to reflect on your progress and adjust accordingly. Only then can you improve yourself consistently and learn to deal effectively with changing circumstances on your journey towards happiness.

Even with all this practical advice on conducting a personal retrospective regularly, it can be daunting to stay motivated, disciplined, and loyal to your intentions of becoming a better and happier version of yourself. Especially for those more challenging situations, there is help nearby in the next chapter, where you will find a maintenance kit stuffed with practical tools and hacks.

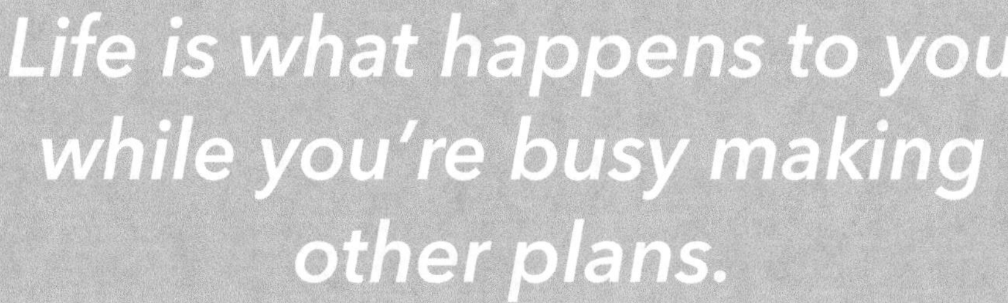

Life is what happens to you while you're busy making other plans.

- John Lennon

Maintenance Kit

By now, you might have the impression that as an experienced Scrum Master I have everything under control and my life is a relaxed sailing trip across smooth waters. Of course, that's not the case. I'm only human and there are times when I lose motivation, get distracted, feel insecure, or become frustrated about lacking results. In those moments when my happiness level is dropping, I realize I need to arrange some extra support for myself. Over the past years, I've collected a few tricks and hacks that proved very helpful.

One of those tricks is tallying. When I noticed I wasn't drinking enough water during the day, I took a new sticky note every day and started tallying each glass of water. That way, I could keep track and remind myself to get myself another glass of water. Another powerful technique I use is success logging, which works like a charm every time I revert to it.

In this chapter, you will learn various techniques to support you when things are not working out as expected or when you feel discouraged. Not everything in life goes as planned, and sometimes there will be setbacks and nasty surprises. When this inevitably happens, it's so easy to focus on what is not going well and forget about the good stuff that is happening. As a result, we get discouraged from investing in what matters to us and our energy level drops. This chapter provides you with some helpful tools when you are looking for extra support to keep on going on your journey toward happiness.

Reminders

In hectic day-to-day life it is quite easy to forget about our priorities, goals and planned actions. Before you know it, you are distracted and potentially wasting your precious time and energy. How about making it easier for yourself to stay loyal to your intentions? Here are some hacks that come in handy to remind yourself to stay on course.

Note to self

Sticky notes are a Scrum Master's best friend. You can use them for personal reminders too of course. Here are a few examples of how that could work in practice.

What could be helpful to write on a sticky note:

- Your purpose.
- The most important task for today (or this week).
- A personal value that you want to express more.
- A particular goal that requires your focus.
- A particular behavior that you want to practice explicitly.
- ...and anything else that matters to you...

Depending on the type of reminder that you want to set up for yourself, there are lots of places where you may want to put one or more sticky notes to support yourself:

- On the bathroom mirror.
- On your laptop.
- On the refrigerator door.
- On the inside of the front door (so you see it on your way out).
- On the dashboard of your car.
- In your wallet.
- On your mobile phone.

I'm sure there are plenty more places you can think of. Get creative and find out what works for you.

Visuals

Some people are more visually oriented. A meaningful painting, picture or drawing can serve as a powerful reminder. You can either search for something on the internet or create it yourself. If you like to be creative, you can make it very personal and powerful.

A physical visual will typically end up on a wall or on a desk or cupboard. You can use a digital visual as the background image on your computer or mobile phone. You can put a visual anywhere you like as long as you see it often enough to serve as a reminder. Tattoos are another example of visual reminders.

A long time ago, I made a drawing of a big tree standing on its own high on a cliff next to a big lake. It may have looked like a childish drawing to others, but for me, it was a reminder of being strong. It was hanging in our bedroom, so I saw it every morning as I got up. That was a great way to empower me.

Objects

Physical objects can serve as powerful reminders. We can all associate a different meaning to a certain object, so the combinations are unlimited. Sometimes, we receive a personal item from a loved one or inherit it, like a watch or jewelry. That object will have a special meaning for us and trigger a certain memory or emotion. Some people are fond of special gems or rocks and carry them in their pockets. Sculptures are another example of objects that can symbolize something personal and valuable. These are just a few examples. In fact, any object can have a special meaning for somebody, and it's just a matter of personal interpretation.

That guided meditation of navigating a sailing boat that I mentioned earlier was a very strong and empowering mental exercise for me. Later on, when I spotted a small wooden steering wheel at a flea market, I bought it immediately. It hung on the wall next to my desk in my study for many years.

Passwords

One of the best life hacks I learned was to use your computer password as a reminder. Enter your most important goal or behavior as the password, and you'll be reminded every time you have to unlock your computer. For a while, I had a password like PublishMyBook2023! Imagine typing that in multiple times per day. For sure, it will remind you!

Success logging

It felt like a rough ride when I started in a new leadership role back in 2022. Despite getting great support, I found it quite overwhelming in the first months, with a lot of new people, processes, and systems to get familiar with. There were a few occasions when I wondered what I had gotten into. Was this new role living up to my expectations? My energy level dropped, and it also started to impact my private life. Then I remembered a helpful routine I once learned many years ago: success logging. This technique has served me many times in the past.

Theory

We often believe we are only successful when we reach the final goal, but all the smaller steps towards our goal are worth acknowledging too. The purpose of success logging is to make us aware of these smaller steps that we so easily take for granted or overlook. This technique helps to find a better and more realistic balance and boosts confidence.

Here is an overview of the various definitions of success:

- **Goal achieved**: You got the job, finished the project, cleaned out the room, ran your first 5K, lost 10 kilograms: achieving a goal you wanted to reach is a success, by definition, for sure. It feels great to accomplish a goal, no matter how big or small. So yes, time to celebrate!

- **Planned action done**: Write a letter, organize a meeting, ask for help, participate in an event, or make a phone call: every goal is reached by completing one or more actions. It is worth acknowledging your commitment to your planned actions. Even if the action didn't lead to the desired result (yet), at least you were loyal to your intentions. Well done!

- **New knowledge or skills acquired**: Training, practicing, studying, and reading: you may need to learn new competencies to be able to progress. This investment in yourself brings you closer to your goal, congrats!

- **New insight gained**: A deeper understanding of yourself or your environment supports you in adapting your plans and actions to meet your goals. Appreciate these moments of wonderful wisdom!

- **Failure acknowledged**: Failing is part of being successful, so it is helpful to identify when something went wrong (=when the result was different than expected). We all make mistakes but are not used to talking about them. Our judgment about failure holds us back. As long as you learn from failure, it serves as a valuable lesson. So, start embracing your failures and the lessons learned. Smile and move on.

Practice

Now it is time to apply these definitions and identify the various shapes and forms of success that you often overlook. Take a piece of paper or a notebook and write down as many successes as you can think of. Aim for at least 10–15, maybe even complete a whole page! It may seem difficult at first, but once you get started, you will find distinguishing the various shapes of success becomes easier. You will be surprised how many successes you can identify in a short timeframe.

When you carry out this routine for a few days in a row, you feel more grateful for everything you do. You can keep on logging successes for as long as you like and experience the benefits of the exercise. You will start to recognize all the steps you are taking toward your goals, which is fun to do because you learn to appreciate the small stuff and everything you took for granted previously. It becomes easier to recognize personal and professional successes in your daily life more naturally.

I hope you find this routine useful. It helped me to find my balance in my new role. It also made me kinder in my self-judgment and more realistic in my ambitions, which helped too.

TIP

Try it for at least one week and observe what happens. It helps to make it a daily routine at a fixed time or place. Even when you only have a few minutes to spare, it will be worth it.

Journaling

Sometimes you run into these tough issues that keep you preoccupied for days or even weeks. You can't wrap your head around it and are desperate for understanding. Maybe it requires taking an important decision. Talking to friends could be helpful, but sometimes you first want to make some sense of things yourself.

Journaling is a very powerful technique to get clarity for yourself by confiding your thoughts to paper. I have used it numerous times, for instance, when I got frustrated about not losing weight, when I struggled in a relationship, when I found myself in a troublesome work situation, or when I needed to explore alternate career options. Journaling can help with any burning issue that keeps you distracted.

Theory

Journaling is a great way to get your head cleared and dump your thoughts on paper. It's self-reflection by writing. All you need is a pen, paper, and some time on your own. If you want to tackle a persistent tough issue, then half an hour would be a minimum on that occasion. If you want to make it a daily habit, then ten minutes per day should be fine. The writing helps to articulate your thoughts. Because you are making your thoughts visible, you challenge yourself to be honest and to the point. By putting your thoughts on paper, you separate yourself from your thoughts. You are not your thoughts.

Practice

Take a piece of paper or a clean page in a notebook. Start by writing down the issue that is bothering you. Put it down as a dilemma or a question to invite yourself to answer.

From here it's just plain writing without hesitation. Let your thoughts flow through your pen onto the paper. Describe the issue as completcly as possible, as if you are explaining the situation to somebody you can fully trust and who will not judge you.

Write down what you think and feel about this issue. Be as complete as possible, covering the different perspectives that come to mind. Try to keep up with your line of thought. Don't waste time on writing beautifully. Nobody needs to read it; this is for you. Also, don't judge your thoughts, give them the attention they deserve and see where they take you next.

When your mind runs dry for a moment, take a second to digest what you have written so far:

- What else comes to mind?
- What does this tell you?
- How does it make you feel?

Your thoughts will start flowing again, so get ready to continue writing.

Eventually, you will come to a point where you have put everything on paper that you could think of. It is very likely that you have gained some new insights by now. It is time to round up:

- What have you learned?
- What do you conclude?
- And last but not least: what are you going to do next?

Power retro

I have been working on my health quite seriously in recent years, and my weight was one of my concerns. So, every morning I stepped onto the scale and logged my meals in an app. In the beginning I succeeded in losing a few kilograms, but eventually I got stuck at a certain weight. I noticed that I was doing well during the work week, but at the weekend I would regain that lost weight. I invented a simple routine to learn on a daily basis. Every day I looked back to assess what behavior had served me the day before. I formulated that lesson as a short positive mantra and logged it in a notes app on my mobile phone. That resulted in phrases like 'stick to your own plate', 'enough is good', 'get creative with lunch', etc. Much to my surprise, I noticed that I finally broke that invisible barrier and my weight finally dropped below 90 kg.

Theory

The key to continuous improvement is learning, from success as well as failure. Conducting a weekly retro is already an effective evaluation routine to inspect and adapt how you are doing. However, sometimes it might not be frequent enough. When you want to learn faster, you need to evaluate more frequent so you can adapt quicker to the latest insights. It is all about shorting the feedback loop.

Practice

Choose a particular goal that you want to focus on with this power retro technique. Select a convenient timeslot that you can stick to on a daily basis. Maybe that is during breakfast, during your daily commute, or just before going to bed. A 5–10 minute timeslot should suffice.

Follow these steps:

- **Inspect**: think back on your actions in the last 24 hours.
- **Choose**: which action impacted your goal the most (positively or negatively)?
- **Positive impact**: condense that action into a personal power quote.
- **Negative impact**: reframe the action into a lesson: what should you have done instead? Or what would have helped to avoid this situation? Formulate this insight into a personal power quote.

It helps to write these power quotes down somewhere to materialize your learning. Just thoughts can be too fluid. When you carry out this technique for some time, you end up with a list of strong and hopefully inspiring statements that will support you in reaching your goal.

Because every day you write down a new power quote, you invest in making insights explicit. It lets you catch up on the previous lessons too.

Music

Music is a mighty instrument to boost morale. A friend of mine shared his personal practice with me. He found that he had developed into a person showing mainly rational and analytical behavior over time, which he calls a walking head. He wanted to return to his original character, being sensitive, having feelings, and showing empathy.

So, he set up a personal playlist called "Rob's Warrior with Feelings." On that list, he put just songs that give him the chills, songs that really touch him in a way that they contain both powerful beats and rhythms and nerve-activating lyrics, sounds, or effects. Whenever he notices that he is spending too much time in his head, he switches to his playlist. After a while, he started noticing that he had grown more sensitive to more pieces of music. And so, his playlist is evolving, just like he is. Music can be a powerful instrument to restore a better balance in life.

Rewards

We can all use some encouragement along the way. So, make a list of fun activities that you can pick from to reward yourself when you feel you could use some extra motivation to keep going. Aim to fill this list with concrete and easy-to-execute actions so you can comfortably pick something on the fly.

Here are some examples:

- Take a 15-minute break.
- Watch some funny animal videos.
- Sit outside and enjoy the sun.
- Have a chat with a friend or colleague about some fun topic.
- Read a chapter in your favorite book.
- Play your favorite song on maximum volume and sing/dance along.
- Treat yourself to a nice lunch.
- Order your favorite pizza or sushi or whatever you love to eat.

Anything enjoyable can be on this list, so pick an item whenever you need a boost. You can also use the list to pick a reward to motivate yourself to complete a particular activity you dread.

Self-care

Even when we are committed to reaching our goals and putting in our best effort, there will be moments when we are unsuccessful and happiness is out of sight. Of course, we can step up our game and try even harder. It is very easy to put pressure on ourselves or feel pressure from others, yet sometimes another approach may be more beneficial. Taking it down a notch may sound counterintuitive, but it could be critical to keep going sustainably in the long run. Here are some self-care tips for you to recuperate at your convenience.

Meditation

Meditation is a way to find inner peace, reduce stress, and boost your overall wellbeing. Through meditation you can learn to manage your emotions and foster positivity, empathy, and compassion. Meditation can even boost your immune system, lower blood pressure, and improve sleep quality.

Here are some first steps to get started if you are new to meditation:

- Find a quiet space where you won't get disturbed.
- Get in a comfortable position, sitting or lying down.
- Start with just 5-10 minutes a day.
- Close your eyes if that feels okay for you.
- Take deep, slow breaths.
- Focus on your breath traveling through your body.
- Your mind may wander, which is perfectly normal. When that happens, gently guide your focus back to your breath and continue.

I've only recently started experimenting with meditation, and I like it a lot, although it is not a regular habit yet. I take 10 minutes after breakfast to listen to a guided meditation talk. For beginners like me, guided meditations are fantastic. You can find apps, podcasts, or YouTube videos leading you through the process. Afterward, I feel more centered, happy, and ready to start a brand-new day.

Power nap

Power naps are the secret weapon for a quick energy boost and mood improvement. A power nap can rejuvenate your energy, helping you feel more alert and focused. It provides a quick mental break, reduces stress and tension, and boosts productivity and creative thinking. Nowadays, even employers have started acknowledging the benefits: workplace napping is becoming more and more accepted, so why wouldn't you apply this for self-care? It has become even easier now that working from home is more common.

I will openly confess that I have embraced the occasional power nap, particularly after lunch when working from home. I'm lucky because I can sleep almost anywhere and doze off in a minute.

Here are some tips on napping from the expert:

- Find a quiet and comfortable place to nap.
- Keep it short to avoid grogginess (10-20 minutes max).
- Set an alarm to make sure you don't oversleep.
- Try to stick to a consistent moment in the day.

Take a walk

Walking is a wonderfully simple and accessible way to improve your health and wellbeing. It is a great way to boost cardiovascular health, maintain a healthy weight, and strengthen your muscles. It's a simple but effective stress reliever that can uplift your mood. It can also improve the quality of your sleep. The best part is that almost anyone can do it, regardless of age or fitness level.

Here are some practical tips:

- Wear comfortable clothing and shoes, dress for the weather.
- Find a nice route that you can enjoy.

- Keep it short and sweet: a 20–30 minute walk will already be beneficial.

- Use this time to clear your mind, listen to music, or simply appreciate the outdoors.

- Bring water if you go on longer walks.

In summer, when the sun rises early, I like to go out for a walk instead of doing a yoga session. We live near a river, and I love that landscape with meadows and trees. When there is enough time, I sit down on the riverbank and just stare at the water slowly passing by. That's sheer happiness for me.

Reading

Reading is a journey of the mind. Reading exercises your brain and keeps your mind sharp. Immersing yourself in a good book can be a great escape from daily stress. Regular reading can enhance your ability to focus. It also exposes you to new words and writing styles, improving your language skills.

Here are some tips to enjoy reading:

- Choose genres and topics that genuinely interest you.

- Create a comfortable, well-lit place to read with minimal distractions.

- Pick a specific time for reading, whether in the morning or before bed, daily or weekly.

- Allow yourself a minimal reading timeframe, even if it's only 10 minutes. At least you get started. Once you start enjoying it more and more, you'll find it easier to allocate more time to your new hobby.

Although I love to hold physical books, I finally spoiled myself with an e-reader and a digital bookshop subscription. It is easier now to pick and read books because the e-reader can hold so many. I've created my own little reading space in an empty corner of our living room, so the opportunity is there when I want to use it. I haven't found a dedicated reading timeslot yet. For me, reading is more of an ad hoc self-care moment that I cherish.

Wellness

Visiting a wellness resort can be a fantastic opportunity to rejuvenate your body, mind, and spirit. Wellness resorts offer a peaceful escape, allowing you to unwind and de-stress. Depending on the facilities, you can also enjoy spa treatments. Wellness resorts often provide good food, making the stay even more comfortable.

Here are a few tips for an optimal wellness resort visit:

- Research and select a wellness resort that aligns with your needs and preferences. You might need to check out a few resorts before you find your favorite.
- Keep in mind that it can be busy during certain days and times in the week.
- Book your stay and any treatments to secure your preferred schedule.
- Take your time to fully enjoy the whole experience, including the trip there and back.

My partner and I enjoy wellness and found our favorite wellness resort. Although it is popular and near a major city, you hardly ever notice how busy it actually is. We usually go in the afternoon and stay until the evening. There is plenty of time to read. Sweating it out in a sauna is a mindful exercise by itself, and I know for sure that I will enjoy an occasional nap when relaxing in between sessions. So, a trip to a wellness center is the ultimate self-care treatment for me.

Summary

In this chapter, you learned various techniques that help you stay focused on your goals and remain loyal to your intentions. Feel free to experiment to determine which technique works for you in a particular situation. In my experience, these techniques are beneficial until you get back on course and no longer need them, and that's just fine. It's reassuring to have some techniques like this in your maintenance kit to fall back on when looking for extra support. Use them whenever you want to, and take good care of yourself.

With your maintenance kit packed with various supporting techniques, you are well-prepared to embark on your journey to happiness. It is time to raise the sails in the next and final chapter.

A ship in the harbor is safe, but that is not what ships are built for.

- John A. Shedd

Happy sailing

You have reached the final chapter. In the previous chapters, I have shared with you the essential tools and practices that I found useful in taking control of your life while navigating life's complexities.

You learned how to create your personal Steering Wheel, with your Purpose as your north star in the chapter ´Steering towards happiness´. Combined with the other sections like Roles, Goals, Values, Behavior, Strengths, Weaknesses, Growth and Needs, the picture of who you are and what you stand for is complete. Through the Steering Wheel, you have control over how you want to organize your life so you can respond to everything that comes your way.

In the chapter ´Planning your journey´, you learned about the Journey Planner, an effective tool for planning your actions on a daily, weekly, and monthly basis to achieve your goals. The chapter ´Mapping your priorities´ provided various techniques to choose how to prioritize your actions and roles. These techniques serve you to create focus on the most valuable and essential actions.

Because life is full of surprises and not everything will go as planned, you learned various techniques to inspect how you are doing and adapt if needed in the chapter 'Checking your course'. The retrospective routine is a very powerful mechanism to help you stay loyal to your goals, values, and purpose.

In the chapter 'Maintenance Kit', I provided you with a care package for those occasions when you could use some extra support. Feel free to use it whenever you like. We are all human with stronger and weaker moments, and sometimes you just need a bit of extra help to keep on going.

A few final words of advice before departure...

The tools and practices presented in this book are suggestions based on my personal experience. You don't have to adapt all of these before you can reap any benefits. You may discover that figuring out your purpose is enough motivation already to get you going, or that the prioritizing and planning practices provide enough structure and process in your life right now.

Maybe you feel a bit overwhelmed after reading this book, and you don't know where to start. Or maybe, you are very busy, and time is scarce. In that case, I'd recommend starting with a personal retrospective regularly. Just ask yourself these two questions: 1) What went well? and 2) What do I want to change? This basic form of self-reflection will give you some first insights to act upon. By doing so, you start a habit of investing in yourself, which is always valuable.

It took me several years to figure out what worked and what didn't for me, and I'm still making some tweaks every now and again. For you, it will be no different. Start the experiment and experience how it works for you, what you like, and what doesn't add value. Use the tools and practices as a starting point at best and take it from there. The best

tools and practices are the ones that you use because they support you
in your life.

Well, your boat is ready to sail. I wish you all the best and a safe passage.
Make sure to enjoy your journey as you navigate the sea of life. Good
luck and happy sailing!

Kind regards,

Herman / Scrumpy Dad

For more information, please visit **www.scrumpydad.com** where you
will find ready-to-use templates, inspiring blogs and other offerings.
Here you can also subscribe to the weekly Scrumpy Dad newsletter.

Feel free to follow me on LinkedIn: **linkedin.com/in/hjameeuwsen/**

Acknowledgements

Although writing a book can be a lonely activity for the author, it requires the support of many people who contribute to the creation process. I want to mention a few of them here, because I am very grateful how they have helped me achieve this big personal goal of mine.

First of all, I'd like to thank my followers on Medium and LinkedIn. I enjoyed all your reactions online and offline on my posts which showed me there was an audience out there eager to learn and get inspired. You fueled my writing engine, so thank you.

A big thank you goes to Linda Haak, Femke Hille, Brian Kemble, Maryse Meinen, Rob Paeper, and Mike Pruis. They were my review team from the start; they diligently reviewed the individual chapters and completed the surveys I sent them. Thank you folks, for being critical in sharing your feedback and cheering me on to keep going. Your involvement and support have been awesome!

Next, I want to thank Ameesha Green and Gemma Rowlands. Ameesha reviewed the manuscript and not only highlighted some crucial improvements, but she also provided many valuable writing suggestions and advice on self-publishing. Gemma went through the manuscript as a proofreader and improved the flow of my sentences. Thank you both for your professional help in taking my book to the next quality level.

A special word of appreciation to Evelien Acun-Roos, Erik de Bos, Linda Bovaird, Maarten Dalmijn, Carsten Lützen, Jeremy Randall, Rini van Solingen, and Gunther Verheyen. All of you responded without hesitation to my request to review my book, although many of you I never met in person before. To me that shows the power of our community, full of wonderful people who are keen to help each other out. I appreciate your help a lot, thank you!

An exceptional big thank you to my friend Peter Kuyt from Visual Friday, who helped me with beautiful illustrations and creative ideas on designing and marketing the first Scrumpy Dad book. All credits for the amazing look & feel of the book go to him. We've had many productive and fun sessions at our kitchen table and later in our favorite café in Utrecht. Thank you for all your help and friendship, Peter, I couldn't have done it without you!

Our kids Maaike, Bart, and Valerie made me a Scrumpy Dad and not just Scrumpy. Thank you for your trust and openness in letting me help you on your personal journeys as adolescents by trying out new methods and applying plenty of sticky notes. I am very proud of you and love you dearly.

Finally, I want to thank my loving and caring wife, Catharina. You coined the term Scrumpy, which has stuck with me ever since. Many evenings, I excused myself and went to my study to continue writing on this book. Thank you for your everlasting support throughout this lengthy project. You gave me the freedom to achieve this big personal goal of mine, and I'm forever grateful. I look forward to spending more quality time together again, with or without sticky notes.

References

1. Schwaber K, Sutherland J, *The Scrum Guide*, www.scrumguides. org, 2020.

2. Beck K, Beedle M, Bennekum A van, et al., *Manifesto for Agile Software Development*, www.agilemanifesto.org, 2001.

3. Ivanov A, Voloshchuk M, *The Team Canvas*, www.theteamcanvas. com, 2015.

4. García H, *Ikigai: The Japanese Secret to a Long and Happy Life*, Hutchinson, 2017.

5. Covey SR, *The 7 Habits of Highly Effective People*, Fireside Books, 2004.

6. Tigchelaar M, *Focus AAN/UIT*, Spectrum, 2019.

7. Bonaker Z, *Seeing the System with the WADE Matrix*, blog post on ScatterSpoke, 2019 (https://www.scatterspoke.com/post/seeing-the-system-with-the-wade-matrix).

8. Hengst M, Hollander den K, *De Mijne zijn de Liefste*, In de wolken, 2019.

Inspiration

Here you will find a selection of resources that I found inspirational on my journey over the past years. I hope you find something interesting that serves you equally well.

Agile and Scrum

Books

Adkins L, *Coaching Agile Teams*, Addison-Wesley, 2010.

Dalmijn M, *Driving Value with Sprint Goals*, Addison-Wesley, 2023.

Solingen van R, *De Bijenherder*, Uitgeverij Business Contact, 2016.

Thoren P, *Agile People*, Lion Crest, 2017.

Verheyen G, *Scrum - A Pocket Guide*, Van Haren Publishing BV, 2013.

Verwijs C, Schartau J, Overeem B, *Zombie Scrum Survival Guide*, Addison-Wesley, 2021.

Retrospective formats

Fun retrospectives: *www.funretrospectives.com*

Retromat: *www.retromat.org*

People to follow on LinkedIn

Carsten Lützen (*also on YouTube*)

Mike Cohn (*www.mountaingoatsoftware.com*)

The Liberators (*www.theliberators.com*)

Coaching

Books

Heller P, *Essential Psychology for Modern Organizations*, Patrick Heller, 2020.

Pink D, Drive, *Canongate Books Ltd.*, 2011.

Pluijm van der S, Coachen 3.0 (reeks), Het Boekenschap, 2018-2021.

Rosenberg M, *Nonviolent Communication*, PuddleDancer Press, 2015.

Veraart-Maas H, *Socratisch Coachen*, Uitgeverij Nelissen, 2006.

Wiss E, *Socrates op Sneakers*, Ambo|Anthos, 2020.

Personal leadership

Books

Clear J, *Atomic Habits*, Random House Business Books, 2015.

Cleese J, *Creativity*, Pinguin Books, 2022.

Coppenhagen R, *Altijd al iets van plan?*, Scriptum, 2004.

Covey SR, *The 8th Habit*, Simon & Schuster, 2006.

Kroon van der T, *De Terugkeer van de Koning*, AnkhHermes, 2021.

Millman D, *Way of the Peaceful Warrior*, New World Library, 1980.

Pirsig R M, *Zen and the Art of Motorcycle Maintenance*, Bantam Books, 1974.

Semler R, *The Seven-Day Weekend*, Cornerstone, 2004.

Tiggelaar B, *Dit wordt jouw jaar!*, Tyler Roland Press, 2011.

Tolle E, *The Power of Now*, Hachette Collections, 2001.

Tuitert M, DRIVE, Maven Publishing, 2021.

Tzu S, *The Art of War*, Arcturus, 2016.

Productivity

Books

Allen D, *Getting things done*, Little, Brown Book Group, 2001.

Bruns M, Postema M, *Maak het af*, Business Contact, 2022.

Loo van der L, *Energy Boost*, Van Duuren Management, 2013.

Pastoor R, *Grip*, Uitgeverij Nz, 2019.

People to follow on LinkedIn

Ben Tiggelaar

Greg McKeown

Kate Sotsenko